CityPack
Chicago

MICK SINCLAIR

Mick Sinclair is a frequent visitor to the US, and has made a career of homing in on the nooks and crannies of America's largest cities. Mick is the author of CityPack San Francisco, *and of AA* Explorer California *and* Explorer New York.

Sears tower
boat ride - evening
Planitanain

City-centre map continues on inside back cover

AA Publishing

Contents

About this book

ORGANISATION

CityPack Chicago's six sections cover the six most important aspects of your visit to Chicago:

- Chicago life – the city and its people
- Itineraries, walks and excursions – how to organise your time
- The top 25 sights to visit, numbered 1–25 from west to east across the city
- Features about different aspects of the city that make it special
- Detailed listings of restaurants, hotels, shops and nightlife
- Practical information

In addition, text boxes provide fascinating extra facts and snippets, highlights of places to visit and invaluable practical advice.

CROSS-REFERENCES

To help you make the most of your visit, cross-references, indicated by ▶, show you where to find additional information about a place or subject.

MAPS

- **The fold-out map** in the wallet at the back of the book is a comprehensive street plan of Chicago. All the map references given in the book refer to this map. For example, the Chicago Board of Trade on W Jackson Boulevard has the following information: ➕ 67 – indicating the grid square of the map in which the Chicago Board of Trade will be found.
- **The city-centre maps** found on the inside front and back covers of the book itself are for quick reference. They show the Top 25 Sights, described on pages 24–48, which are clearly plotted by number (**1** – **25**, not page number) from west to east.

PRICES

Where appropriate, an indication of the cost of an establishment is given by **£** signs: **£££** denotes higher prices, **££** denotes average prices, while **£** denotes lower charges.

CHICAGO *life*

INTRODUCING CHICAGO

Looking up at the El

Re-named El lines

During the mid-1990s, Chicago's confusingly named El (elevated railway) lines were retitled with easier to understand colour codes. However, you are still likely to hear the old names, which usually refer to the end points of each route:

Green – Lake/Englewood/ Jackson Park

Brown – Ravenswood/Loop

Red – Howard/Dan Ryan

Purple – Linden /Howard (rush hours only)

Blue – O'Hare/Congress/ Douglas

Orange – Midway Airport

Towering buildings, a lake reaching to the horizon, the rumble of El trains, the raising of hot-dogs to an art form, and weather that can change at the drop of a hat, are all facets of Chicago – the great city of the American Midwest, internationally celebrated as a showplace of world-class building and design. From Frank Lloyd Wright to Miles van der Rohe, every major modern architect has left a calling card in the 'Windy City'.

The architectural pedigree stems from a three-day fire in 1871, after which Chicago had to be built afresh. New steel-frame construction techniques, the invention of the lift, and the booming city's need to make as much use as possible of a single plot of land, conspired to make Chicago the first city of skyscrapers. With their 20-storey office blocks and department stores, design pioneers such as Daniel Burnham and Louis Sullivan – leading what became known worldwide as the Chicago School of Architecture – gave Chicago a unique skyline. A surprising number of early structures remain, among them the Carson Pirie Scott & Co Store, the Rookery and the Reliance Building, their terracotta façades overshadowed by the soaring glass and steel edifices that now sprout from the Loop – Chicago's business district. The technological ingenuity that enabled steadily higher construction climaxed in 1974 with the 110-storey Sears Tower.

A quote of unknown origin labelled Chicago 'the city that works'. The fact is Chicago *has* to work, although few people seem to appreciate its crucial role as one of the dynamos driving the nation. Being the hub of transport and trade between the US's east and west contributed to its fast-paced growth through the 19th century. The city remains the major marketplace for the multi-million dollar agricultural produce of the American Midwest, and a venue for scores of major trade shows and conventions. Chicago's O'Hare Airport is one of the world's busiest air terminals, so when heavy snows close the runways air travel across much of the US is paralysed.

When it's not working hard, Chicago plays hard. The city has spawned football legends, such as the Chicago Bears' Mike Ditka, and basketball superstars such as the Chicago Bulls' Michael Jordan. North Side basketball fans cheer the National League Chicago Cubs playing on real grass at historic Wrigley Field, while their counterparts watch the American League White Sox on the astroturf of Comiskey Park.

Like the archetypal American city, Chicago's growth has been the result of waves of immigration. Irish, Italians, Poles and Germans were among the early arrivals from Europe whose labour contributed to the expansion of the city and whose presence is still apparent. St Patrick's Day is one of the city's major annual festivals, and Chicago is one of the few US cities where it is not surprising to hear Ukrainian being spoken on the street. Among the African-Americans who came from the Deep South were the musicians that created the distinctive style of the Chicago blues and those that helped make the city a place of pilgrimage for the world's jazz fans.

Today's Chicago continues to be shaped by new arrivals, with growing Hispanic enclaves – long-established Mexican-Americans were joined

Celebrity restaurants

Chicago's many eating places (► 62–9) include several where the host has a fame unconnected with gastronomy. Among them are Michael Jordan's (✉ 500 N La Salle Street), opened by the basketball star; Harry Caray's (✉ 33 W Kinzie Street), owned by the legendary announcer at the Chicago Cubs' Wrigley Field; and The Eccentric (✉ 159 W Erie Street), belonging to Chicago-based TV sob-and-tell pioneer Oprah Winfrey.

The Downtown skyline, seen across Grant Park

Studs Terkel

Born in New York in 1912, Studs Terkel arrived in Chicago as a child and later established himself as one of the city's most listened-to radio interviewers. Terkel's trademark style of allowing the interviewee to tell his or her own story largely unhindered continued into a string of internationally acclaimed books of oral history, among them *Division Street: America*, describing Chicago through the words of 70 of its citizens.

through the 1970s and 1980s by arrivals from Central America – and recent waves of immigration from India, Korea, Thailand and other parts of Southeast Asia. All settlers, past or present, find that Chicago makes demands. Climate alone necessitates an all-weather wardrobe almost all year round. Another necessity is an understanding of the strange ability of the Chicago Cubs and the White Sox to be unsuccessful season after season (the Cubs last won the World Series in 1908, the White Sox in 1917), while the basketball and football fraternities bask in glory.

In return, Chicago offers a horde of first-rate museums (among them the Chicago Historical Society and the Art Institute of Chicago), cultural activity rarely bettered elsewhere in the country, and Magnificent Mile shops that not only rival those of New York but are gathered in a succession of architecturally inventive retail centres. Beaches belie the fact that Chicago is almost a thousand miles from the nearest ocean, and a nine-month-long programme of major events takes place for free in the city's parks.

With few of the social status hang-ups found in New York or Los Angeles, Chicagoans appear refreshingly straightforward and friendly. A broad rivalry exists between North and South Siders, but more revealing is the

Street art: a tiled mural livens up the Loop

fact that Chicago splits into 77 neighbourhoods, each with its own looks and atmosphere. The abiding impression is that Chicagoans do not live in a city at all but in close-knit communities in a dense conglomeration of small towns – part of a metropolitan area that locals, without a trace of whimsy, refer to as 'Chicagoland'.

CHICAGO IN FIGURES

GENERAL INFORMATION

- Miles from London: 4,167
- Miles from Berlin: 4,793
- Miles from New York: 724
- Miles from San Francisco: 1,756
- Population: 2.78 million; third-largest city in US
- Area: 228$\frac{1}{2}$sq miles
- Miles of street: 3,676
- Miles of lake front: 29
- Miles of beaches: 15
- Miles of lake-front bicycle paths: 18
- Parks: 552

GEOGRAPHY

- Latitude: N 41° 50'
- Longitude: W 87° 45'
- Highest point: 672ft above sea-level

LAKE MICHIGAN

- Length: 321 miles
- Width: 118 miles
- Shoreline: 1,638 miles
- Average depth: 279ft
- Greatest depth: 923ft

ARCHITECTURE

- Tallest buildings: Sears Tower (1,454ft); Amoco Building (1,136ft); John Hancock Center (1,127ft)
- Building with largest floor space: the Merchandise Mart, 90 acres
- Moveable bridges: 50

WEATHER

- Hottest day recorded: 105°F, 24 July 1934
- Coldest day recorded: -27°F, 20 January 1985
- Fastest wind gust recorded: 69mph, 29 April 1984
- Windiest months: March and April
- Wettest month: June
- Hottest month: July

TRIVIA

- Chicago's Lyon & Healy are the world's oldest makers of standing string harps
- Chicago's Nabisco has the world's largest biscuit and cracker factory, at 7300 S Kedzie Avenue
- Chicago's firm of William Wrigley Jr is the world's biggest manufacturer of chewing-gum

A CHRONOLOGY

1673	Jacques Marquette and Louis Joliet discover the 1½-mile Native American portage trail linking the Mississippi River and the Great Lakes – the site of future Chicago
1779–81	Trapper and trader Jean-Baptiste Point Du Sable, a Haitian of African and French descent, becomes the first non-native settler
1812	Fort Dearborn, one of several forts protecting trade routes, is attacked by Native Americans (allied with the British, with whom the US is at war). Some 50 of its occupants die
1830	Chicago is selected as the site of a canal linking the Great Lakes and the Mississippi
1850	Chicago's population reaches 30,000 (300 in 1830). Many arrivals are Irish, who find work building the Midwest's railways
1870	Chicago's population reaches 300,000
1871	The Great Fire (▶ 12). Rebuilding endows Chicago with many notable structures and a reputation as an architectural showplace
1886	The 'Haymarket Riot' (▶ 12). At a worker's rally, police open fire on the crowd. The trial and executions that follow are condemned by labour movements worldwide
1893	Chicago hosts the World's Columbian Exposition. The hyperbole of business leaders encourages a visiting journalist to describe Chicago as 'the windy city', an enduring epithet
1894	A strike at the Pullman rail company unites black and white workers for the first time
1906	Upton Sinclair's novel, *The Jungle*, focuses national attention on the conditions endured by workers in the Union Stockyards, a notorious slaughterhouse and packing complex
1908	Chicago Cubs win baseball's World Series for a

second successive year, following the success of the Chicago White Sox in 1906

1914 With World War I, Chicago's black population increases further as African-Americans from the Deep South move north to industrial jobs

1919–33 Prohibition. Excellent transportation links make Chicago a natural centre for alcohol manufacture and distribution. Armed crime mobs thrive

1950s In South Side clubs, rhythmic and electrified 'Chicago blues' evolves. Muddy Waters and John Lee Hooker are prime exponents

1955 Richard J Daley is elected mayor and serves six terms, dominating Chicago political life for 21 years

1968 Police attack Anti-Vietnam War protesters in Grant Park during the Democratic National Convention, an event seen on TV by millions

1974 Completion of Sears Tower, the world's tallest building until 1996

Late 1980s DJs at Chicago's Warehouse nightclub create 'house music', characterised by digital sampling, cross-fading and hard 'techno' beats, inspiring a worldwide dance-music explosion

1989 Richard M Daley, son of Richard J, is elected mayor

1991 The Chicago Bulls win basketball's NBA Championship, the first of many successes inspired by Michael Jordan

1992 A collapsing wall causes the Chicago River to flood into the Loop, paralysing the business district for two weeks

1995 A heatwave kills 700 people

1997 Cabbies strike over the law requiring them to pick up all fares and serve all areas of the city

PEOPLE & EVENTS FROM HISTORY

Richard J Daley

With 60,000 jobs in what he dubbed the 'Machine' of the city administration either directly appointed or greatly influenced by him, Richard J Daley (aka 'The Boss') dominated Chicago politics from 1955 until 1976. Daley won the favour of big business but was loathed elsewhere for his autocratic style and readiness to use force, most notoriously against demonstrators at the 1968 Democratic Convention.

Chicago's legendary mobster, Al Capone

THE GREAT FIRE

The summer of 1871 had been exceptionally hot and dry, with many forest fires breaking out in the Chicago area. On 8 October, warm winds caused a fire in the south-west of the city to spread rapidly. Crashing meteors, a dropped match, and a Mrs O'Leary's cow knocking over the lantern in its barn are among the many theories and legends on how the fire started. The fire jumped the Chicago River, and blazed for two days through a city where firefighting personnel and equipment had failed to keep pace with growth. Before it was extinguished by judiciously used gunpowder and the arrival of heavy rain, the fire claimed 250 lives in all, razed nearly 18,000 buildings over four square miles, and rendered over 90,000 people homeless.

THE HAYMARKET RIOT

Heavy-handed police tactics in a series of labour disputes prompted a group of German-born anarchists to organise a protest rally on 4 May 1886 in Haymarket Square. A bomb thrown from the crowd exploded among the police lines; the explosion, and the subsequent police use of firearms, killed seven people and wounded 150. As a result, seven anarchists received death sentences. In 1893, a full pardon was granted to three anarchists serving prison terms, due to the lack of evidence linking any anarchists to the bomb.

GANGSTERS

Intended to encourage sobriety and family life, Prohibition (1919–33), provided a great stimulus to organised crime in the US. The exploits of Chicago-based gangsters such as Al Capone became legendary. Though depicted frequently in films and on TV, shoot-outs between rival gangs were rare. An exception was the 1929 St Valentine Day's Massacre when Capone's gang eliminated their arch-rivals in a hail of machine-gun fire. Wealthy enough to bribe corruptible politicians and police, gangsters seemed invincible, but the gangster-era – though not necessarily the gangs – ended with the imprisonment of Capone, in 1931, and the repeal of Prohibition.

CHICAGO
how to organise your time

ITINERARIES

Chicago is best seen on foot. Walking between neighbourhoods in and around the Loop is safe and easy, although journeys further afield require a car or travel on the city's comprehensive network of buses, El trains and, less often, Metra commuter trains.

ITINERARY ONE	**THE LOOP AND ART INSTITUTE OF CHICAGO**
Morning	Wait for the rush hour to subside and begin a walk around the Loop. Take in the many points of historic and architectural interest: start at Sears Tower, and head steadily eastwards
Lunch	Berghoff Restaurant (► 65) or Russian Tea Café (► 65)
Afternoon	Complete your tour of the Loop and cross into Grant Park (► 41). Spend the rest of the day at the Art Institute of Chicago (► 40) or simply strolling the park. Alternatively, take public transport to the Jane Addams Hull-House Museum (► 26)
ITINERARY TWO	**THE MAGNIFICENT MILE AND VICINITY**
Morning	From the Michigan Avenue Bridge, view the Wrigley Building and Tribune Tower, and then go north past the glitzy shops of the Magnificent Mile (► 51). Tour the Terra Museum of American Art (► 36), then continue to the elegant houses along the Gold Coast (► 50, panel)
Lunch	Gino's East (► 66) or Seasons (► 62)
Afternoon	Continue northward by bus to Lincoln Park (► 29). Spend the rest of the day there, visiting the zoo (► 29 and 59), conservatory, beaches and other attractions, according to your taste and the weather. In the south of the park is the Chicago Historical Society (► 33). Alternatively, return south and spend the afternoon visiting the North Pier and Navy Pier (► 60)

ITINERARY THREE	MAJOR MUSEUMS AND GRACELAND CEMETERY OR WRIGLEY FIELD
Morning	Spend the whole day visiting the Field Museum of Natural History (➤ 42), the John G Shedd Aquarium (➤ 44) and the Adler Planetarium and its astronomical exhibits (➤ 46). All three are excellent for children. Or select one or two of these museums and spend the afternoon as detailed below
Lunch	Soundings Restaurant (➤ 44), or a picnic in Grant Park (➤ 41)
Afternoon	Take public transport south to the University of Chicago campus to visit the Oriental Institute (➤ 47), followed by the Du Sable Museum of African-American History (➤ 45). If you have children with you, the Museum of Science and Industry (➤ 48) is a better stop. Or, take public transport north to tour Graceland Cemetery (➤ 27); or go to watch the Chicago Cubs play at Wrigley Field (➤ 28, April to October – check match times ahead)
ITINERARY FOUR	UKRAINIAN AND POLISH CHICAGO, AND OAK PARK
Morning	Take public transport to the Ukrainian Village (➤ 51). Explore the Village, where you'll find St Nicholas Cathedral (➤ 56), which serves the Ukrainian community, and the Ukrainian Culture Center. Continue to the Polish Museum of America (➤ 25)
Lunch	Saks Ukrainian Village Restaurant (➤ 65) or, at a weekend, Mareva's (➤ 65)
Afternoon	Take public transport to Oak Park. Visit the Frank Lloyd Wright Home & Studio (➤ 24) and Unity Temple (➤ 56), which was also designed by Frank Lloyd Wright. Stroll past the many other buildings of architectural and historic interest in the vicinity, including the birthplace of, and the museum devoted to, writer Ernest Hemingway (➤ 53)

WALKS

Dubuffet's Monument with Standing Beast

INFORMATION

Distance Approx 1½ miles
Time 2–3 hours
Start point Sears Tower
🚇 G7
🚊 Brown and Orange lines: Quincy
🚌 1, 60, 151, 156
End point Chicago Cultural Center
🚇 H6
🚊 Brown and Orange lines: Madison
🚌 3, 4, 60, 145, 147, 151

THE WEST LOOP

Begin at Sears Tower (1974), until recently the world's tallest building, with a fantastic view from its 103rd-floor Skydeck. Continue along Jackson Boulevard for the Chicago Board of Trade (1930), observing the trading from the visitors' gallery. Turn north along La Salle Street and peek inside the architecturally stunning Rookery (1880s). Continue north to the junction with Randolph Street to view the James R Thompson Center (formerly known as the State of Illinois Centre, and built in 1985), which has the controversial Dubuffet sculpture, *Monument with Standing Beast*, looming outside. Inside, the 17-storey atrium echoes the building's curvilinear exterior and allows natural light to flood in. Cross Randolph Street to look inside the Richard J Daley Center (1965). Leave by the Washington Street side to view *Untitled*, the 50ft-tall Picasso sculpture made from 162 tons of steel, its meaning in the imagination of the beholder.

Lunch and snacks Food stands lining the lower level of the James R Thompson Center offer fast food. The Berghoff Restaurant (➤ 65), a Chicago institution, serves hearty German fare. On the ground floor of the Chicago Cultural Center is a café serving good coffee and snacks.

THE EAST LOOP

Stroll south along the increasingly tree-lined State Street, passing the glass and terracotta Reliance Building (1890s). Look out for Miró's sculpture, *Chicago*, marking the plaza of 69 W Washington Street. Continue to Louis Sullivan's exquisite, turn-of-the-century Carson Pirie Scott & Co building, and cross to Dearborn Street for the Marquette Building (1895). Resume walking south for the Harold Washington Library Center. End the walk by strolling north along Michigan Avenue to the Chicago Cultural Center (1897), at the junction with Washington Street.

THE MAGNIFICENT MILE: SOUTH

Leave the Loop by walking north across the Chicago River on Michigan Avenue Bridge, which in 1920 facilitated the rise of the so-called Magnificent Mile as a fashionable retail and commercial area. Two of the first structures erected after the bridge was built were the Wrigley Building (1921/1924), to the left, and the Tribune Tower (1925), to the right. Further north, opulent shops and hotels line Michigan Avenue. One of the liveliest stores is Nike Town, a retail showplace of the sports clothing manufacturer, between Erie and Huron streets. Cross to the west side of Michigan Avenue to see the excellent Terra Museum of American Art.

Lunch The Billy Goat Tavern (➤ 83) offers burgers and similar snacks. Pizzeria Uno (➤ 67, panel) is *the* place for deep-dish pizza. For more exotic fare, try Szechwan East (➤ 68) or the weekday lunch buffet at Bukhara (➤ 68).

THE MAGNIFICENT MILE: NORTH

Continue to the junction with Chicago Avenue and stop at the Visitor Information Center inside the Historic Water Tower (1869), which survived the fire. A block north, on the junction with Chestnut Street, stands the imposing Gothic Fourth Presbyterian Church, often used for lunchtime recitals. A short distance west, on Chestnut Street, there is more Gothic exuberance at the Quigley Seminary (1920s). Return to and cross Michigan Avenue to Water Tower Place, a glitzy, high-profile shopping mall. Across Delaware Place is the Palmolive Building, a 1930 art deco landmark that in the 1950s became the base of the *Playboy* magazine empire. Finish the walk at the John Hancock Center (1970), whose 94th-floor observatory affords stunning views.

THE SIGHTS

- Wrigley Building (➤ 35)
- Tribune Tower (➤ 39)
- Terra Museum of American Art (➤ 36)
- Historic Water Tower (➤ 54)
- Fourth Presbyterian Church (➤ 56)
- Quigley Seminary (➤ 56)
- John Hancock Center (➤ 55)

INFORMATION

Distance 1 mile
Time 2–3 hours
Start point Michigan Ave Bridge
- H5/6
- Red line: Grand
- 3, 11, 29, 65, 147, 151, 157

End point John Hancock Center
- H4
- Red line: Chicago
- 145, 146, 147, 151

View from the John Hancock Center

EVENINGS OUT

An evening in Chicago can span bar-hopping and nightclubbing, listening to live music, or simply strolling the late-opening shops. Several neighbourhoods have reputations for being particularly interesting at night.

City nightlife: the lights of Downtown Chicago

INFORMATION

River North and River West
✚ F/G4/5
🚇 Brown line: Chicago. Red line: Grand, Chicago
🚌 22, 37, 41, 65, 66

Rush and Division streets
✚ G/H4
🚇 Red line: Clark/Division
🚌 36, 70

Wrigleyville/Lake View
✚ Off map to north
🚇 Brown, Red lines: Belmont. Red line: Addison
🚌 22, 36, 77, 151, 152

RIVER NORTH AND RIVER WEST
Immediately north of the Loop, the area called River North holds numerous restaurants that function as nightlife venues as much as they do places to eat. Here are the local branches of Hard Rock Café and Planet Hollywood, and their lesser-known local rivals. Across the Chicago River, where a few old warehouses mark River West, are more top-rated nightspots, though the area is not suited to casual evening strolling.

RUSH AND DIVISION STREETS
Although River North and River West have taken away some of the area's customers, the northern section of Rush Street (close to Division Street), near the Loop and many tourist hotels, is a long-established nightlife area with bars, restaurants, small music venues and dance clubs appealing to a wide age group. The proliferation of nightspots in a compact area makes this a good place to stroll among the throng.

WRIGLEYVILLE/LAKE VIEW
These two neighbourhoods (several miles north of the Loop, but easy to reach by El train or bus), which have increasingly been settled by liberal-minded Chicagoans in their mid-20s and 30s, hold most of the newer and more alternative-minded live-music venues and clubs, as well as all manner of bars and cafés. The city's main concentration of gay and lesbian nightspots is also here. Most activity is along Belmont Avenue, Broadway and Clark Street, and to a lesser extent along Sheffield, Halsted and Lincoln avenues.

ORGANISED SIGHTSEEING

WALKING TOURS

Chicago Architecture Foundation (☎ 312/922 TOUR) Walking tours of the Loop's landmark buildings of North Michigan Avenue and, some Sunday mornings, guided walks through Graceland Cemetery.

BOAT TOURS

Chicago Architecture Foundation (☎ 312/922 3432) A 90-minute narrated boat trip to view the architecturally significant buildings lining the Chicago River.

Chicago's First Lady (☎ 347/358 1330) Narrated voyage past some of the Loop's best architecture, including lunch or dinner; a 'lunch magic' cruise features a magician.

Mercury, Chicago's Skyline Cruiseline (☎ 312/332 1368) A choice of one- to two-hour cruises, some specialising in history or architecture. Includes the Chicago River and Lake Michigan.

Spirit of Chicago (☎ 312/321 1241) Lunch or dinner; or dinner-and-dance trips on Lake Michigan.

BUS TOURS

Chicago Trolley Company (☎ 312/663 0260) and the **Chicago Motor Coach Company** (☎ 312/922 8919) Both operate guided tours in and around the Loop; ticket-holders can hop on and off at marked stops.

Chicago Architecture Foundation (☎ 312/922 3432) A choice of bus tours concentrating on general architectural highlights, the buildings of Frank Lloyd Wright, or historic homes.

Tour Black Chicago (☎ 312/332 2323) Reveals a century of African-American culture in Chicago, concentrating on South Side neighbourhoods such as Bronzeville and the Pullman District.

The Party Bus (☎ 312/266 7330) On Fridays and Saturdays, this double-decker bus ferries its passengers to four Chicago nightclubs; no cover charges or queueing for club entry.

Air tours and carriage rides

One of the few ways to get higher than Chicago's towering buildings is by taking a small plane or helicopter tour. Chicago By Air (☎ 708/524 1172) offers a half-hour swoop above the city in a single-engined plane. By contrast, The Noble Horse (☎ 312/266 7878) provides the chance to ride a horsedrawn buggy along the Magnificent Mile.

Travelling in style along Michigan Avenue

EXCURSIONS

INFORMATION

North Shore

Distance From the Loop: Evanston
12 miles; Wilmette 16 miles;
Chicago Botanic Gardens
25 miles

Journey time Evanston 20–30
minutes; Wilmette 25–35
minutes; Chicago Botanic
Gardens 35–40 minutes

🚉 Evanston or Davis

Block Gallery

✉ Northwestern University,
1967 S Campus Drive,
Evanston

☎ 847/491 4000

🕐 Tue–Wed noon–5;
Thu–Sun noon–8

🎟 Free

Grosse Point Lighthouse

✉ 2601 Sheridan Road,
Evanston

☎ 847/328 6961

🕐 Jun–Sep daily 2–5

🎟 Moderate

Baha'i House of Worship

✉ 100 Linden Avenue,
Wilmette

☎ 847/853 2300

🕐 May–Sep daily 10–10.
Oct–Apr daily 10–5

🚉 Wilmette

🎟 Free

Chicago Botanic Gardens

✉ 1000 Lake-Cook Road,
Glencoe (take I-94 north)

☎ 847/835 5440

🕐 Daily 8AM–sunset

🎟 Moderate

NORTH SHORE

The communities lining Lake Michigan north of Chicago are best toured as a whole by car, though numerous individual places of interest are easily reached by public transportation.

Evanston, Chicago's oldest and largest suburb, has upmarket stores which lure many city-dwellers on weekend buying expeditions, and its two historic districts of 19th-century residences are pleasant. Evanston is also the site of Northwestern University, whose Block Gallery mounts excellent art exhibitions. The lake front immediately north of the university is ideal strolling and picnic territory. Make for the 1873 Grosse Point Lighthouse and enjoy the splendid lake view from its 113ft-high tower.

Continuing north, Wilmette holds the Baha'i House of Worship, built over 40 years from 1920 and the first temple in the United States for this religion, originally from Iran. Mosque-like in appearance, the temple is topped by a voluminous dome. Further north near Glencoe, in the 385-acre Chicago Botanic Gardens, landscaped pathways link carefully nurtured English Rose, Japanese Island and Prairie gardens.

PULLMAN

Built in the 1880s for the 11,000 workers of the Pullman company (known for its railroad cars), Pullman was protected as a National Historic Landmark in 1971, and many of its 1,800 original buildings remain. Take the Metra train to Pullman; by car, take Dan Ryan and Calumet expressways south, exiting to the west at 111th Street.

The creation of the town, although apparently an act of paternalism by company owner George M Pullman, was inspired in part by a wish to keep his workforce away from the influence of Chicago's organised labour movement. Ironically, the company's failure to lower rents in line with wage cuts, among other grievances, led to the celebrated Pullman strike of 1894.

WESTERN SUBURBS

If you have a car, a couple of other attractions are worth your while. Closest is Brookfield Zoo, 14 miles from the city in the town of Brookfield. With 2,500 creatures spread across 215 acres of replicated habitat, including an indoor rain forest, the zoo is enjoyable, particularly for children, but is unlikely to consume more than a few hours. Without youngsters to please, a better stop is the Morton Arboretum, in Lisle, 25 miles from the city. Landscaped woodlands, wetlands and prairie are spread across 1,500 acres criss-crossed by foot trails and a 12-mile road tour route. Further west, via I-88 and State Route 31, the idyllic small towns of St Charles, Geneva and Batavia line the Fox River, each with a generous endowment of antiques shops and preserved historic buildings. Take I-88 then State Route 31.

SIX FLAGS GREAT AMERICA

Gurnee, west of the city, is the home of Six Flags Great America, the Midwest's largest theme park, where in its five historically themed areas you will find spectacular high-rise rollercoasters that reach speeds of 65mph, and other thrill rides – including a few for small children – plus an IMAX theatre. Be sure to sample the Pictorium Theater, where films of action stunts, natural phenomena and much more are projected with frightening realism onto a gigantic screen.

INFORMATION

**Historic Pullman Foundation
Visitors Center**
- ✉ 11141 S Cottage Grove Avenue
- ☎ 773/785 8181

Brookfield Zoo
Distance 14 miles from the Loop
Journey time 20–30 minutes
- ✉ First Avenue and 31st Street, Brookfield
- ☎ 708/485 2200
- 🕐 Sep–May daily 10–4:30. Jun–Aug daily 9:30–5:30
- 💰 Moderate; free Oct–Mar Tue and Thu

Morton Arboretum
Distance 25 miles from the Loop
Journey time 50–60 minutes
- ✉ On State Route 50, Lisle
- ☎ 708/719 2400
- 🕐 Daily 7–7
- 💰 Moderate

Six Flags Great America
Distance 43 miles from the Loop
Journey time 70–90 minutes
- ✉ Gurnee, accessed from I-94 at 132 E Grand Avenue exit
- ☎ 847/249 1776
- 🕐 Late Apr–Aug daily 10–5/6/7/8/9/10. Early Sep Sat–Sun 10–8/9
- 💰 Expensive, but rides included in admission price

WHAT'S ON

Whether it is a major museum exhibition or a neighbourhood get-together, something special is happening in Chicago almost every week of the year. A free quarterly booklet, *Chicago Calendar of Events*, can be picked up at one of the city's three visitor centres (➤ 90). Other sources for what's-on information are the Friday *Chicago Tribune*, *Chicago* magazine and the weekly free newspapers, *Reader* and *New City*.

JANUARY/FEBRUARY	*Chinese New Year*: celebrated in Chinatown
MARCH	*St Patrick's Day*: the whole city, including the Chicago River, turns green, and there's a parade through the Loop
APRIL	*Spring Flower shows*: Lincoln Park and Garfield Park conservatories
MAY	*Polish Constitution Day* (7 May): Chicago's many Polish-Americans celebrate with a parade in the Loop and other events focusing on Polish culture
	Wright Plus: once-a-year chance to see inside private Oak Park homes designed by Frank Lloyd Wright
JUNE	*Chicago Blues Festival*: local and international artists perform for massive audiences in Grant Park
	Printer's Row Book Fair: used-book shops offer bargains and host special events
	Chicago Gospel Festival: gospel music in Grant Park
	Taste of Chicago: a feeding frenzy; in the eight days before 4 July, thousands sample dishes from city restaurants. It ends with a firework display
JULY	*Independence Day* (4 July): special events such as firework displays, the largest taking place in Grant Park
	Ravinia Festival (from mid-June through Labor Day): two months of the Chicago Symphony Orchestra, plays and other cultural events, with picnicking on the lawns
AUGUST	*Chicago Air & Water Show*: spectacular stunts performed off North Avenue Beach
SEPTEMBER	*Chicago Jazz Festival*: international jazz stars headline free concerts in Grant Park
OCTOBER	*Chicago Marathon*: 26-mile run through the city, beginning and ending in Grant Park
NOVEMBER	*Festival of Lights*: 30,000 lights illuminate the Magnificent Mile for the Christmas season

CHICAGO's
top 25 sights

The sights are shown on the maps on the inside front cover and inside back cover, numbered **1–25** *from west to east across the city*

1

FRANK LLOYD WRIGHT HOME & STUDIO

DID YOU KNOW?

- 1867 Frank Lloyd Wright born in Wisconsin
- 1887 Arrives in Chicago
- 1909 Leaves Chicago, spends a year in Europe
- 1910 Opens Taliesin, a home and architectural school in Wisconsin
- 1936 Designs Fallingwater – a family home extending over a natural waterfall in a forest near Pittsburgh – a masterpiece of organic architecture
- 1938 Taliesin West, a winter home and school, opens in Arizona
- 1943 Finishes plans for New York's Guggenheim Museum; completed 16 years later
- 1959 Dies

INFORMATION

- ✚ Off map to west
- ✉ 951 Chicago Avenue, Oak Park
- ☎ 708/848 1976
- ◉ Guided tours only: Mon–Fri 11, 1, 3; Sat– Sun 11–4 continuously
- 🚇 Blue line: Harlem
- 🚌 23
- 🚉 Oak Park
- ♿ Few
- 💲 Moderate
- ↔ Hemingway Museum (▶ 53), Unity Temple (▶ 56)

An insight into the early ideas of one of the greatest and most influential architects of the 20th century. It is an essential stop for anyone interested in design, or in the ability of one man to realise his extraordinary vision.

Organic ideas Working for the Chicago architect Louis Sullivan, the 22-year-old Frank Lloyd Wright designed this home in 1889 for himself, his first wife and their children, and furnished it with his own pieces. The shingled exterior is not typical of Wright but the bold geometric shape stands out among the neighbouring Queen Anne-style houses. Inside, the open plan, central fireplaces and low ceilings are the earliest examples of the elements that became fundamental in Wright's so-called Prairie School of Architecture. Particularly notable are the children's playroom, the high-backed chairs in the dining room, and the willow tree that grows through the walls in keeping with Wright's theory of 'organic architecture' – architecture in harmony with its natural surroundings.

Prairie views In 1893, Wright opened his own practice in an annexe to the house: a concealed entrance leads into an office showcasing many of Wright's ideas, such as suspended lamps and open-plan work space. The draughts-men once employed on seminal Prairie School buildings worked in a stunningly designed room in sight of what was then open prairie.

Frank Lloyd Wright's Draughting Room

POLISH MUSEUM OF AMERICA

While this museum does not record Chicago's Polish community specifically, it does enable many Chicago Poles to trace their roots. It has also provided a secure home for Polish cultural treasures that were threatened during the troubled years that followed World War II.

History East Europeans have long had a strong presence in Chicago, but no group among them has had greater visibility than Polish-Americans. Stanislow Batowski's immense painting, *Pulaski at Savannah*, dominates the museum's main room and sets off the collections remembering Pulaski and Koscziusko, two Polish soldiers who played significant roles in the American Revolution. The former was killed in battle and the latter helped lead the 1794 Polish uprising against Russia. Near by are folk costumes, decorated Easter eggs, the costumes of the celebrated Shakespearean actress Helena Modrzejewska, and remnants of the first Polish church in the United States.

Artistry Modestly occupying a corner is the immense stained-glass window that formed the centrepiece of the Polish culture exhibition at the 1939 New York World's Fair, its return home halted by the outbreak of war in Europe. The stairways and an upper floor are lined by Polish art old and new. Amid many fine graphic works, look out for Mrozewski's cryptic 1936 depiction of H G Wells. A separate room has mementoes of Ignaczi Jan Paderewski, the pianist and composer whose concert tours of the US raised funds in the struggle for Polish independence in the early 1900s and who, in 1919, became the first prime minister of the Polish Republic. The last piano on which Paderewski performed is here, and so is the chair he used for all his performances.

DID YOU KNOW?

- 1851 Anton Smarzewski becomes Chicago's first Polish settler
- 1864 Peter Kiolbasa arrives in Chicago from Texas; entering public life, he becomes the city's first well-known Polish-American; he is nicknamed 'honest Pete'
- 1869 Chicago's first Roman Catholic parish is established by Polish settlers
- 1871 German oppression of Poles causes a great rise in emigration to the US. Many settle in Chicago
- 1920 Poles become Chicago's largest foreign-born ethnic group
- 1937 Polish Museum opens

INFORMATION

- E4
- 984 N Milwaukee Avenue
- 773/384 3352
- Daily 11–4
- Blue line: Division
- 9, 41, 56
- Few
- Donation requested
- Ukrainian Village (► 51)

3

JANE ADDAMS HULL-HOUSE MUSEUM

DID YOU KNOW?

- 1860 Jane Addams born in Cedarville, Illinois
- 1888 Visits England
- 1889 Opens Hull House with college friend Ellen Gates Starr
- 1909 Helps founding of National Association for Advancement of Colored People (NAACP)
- 1920 Helps founding of American Civil Liberties Union
- 1931 First American woman to receive Nobel Peace Prize
- 1935 Dies

INFORMATION

- F7
- 800 S Halsted Street
- 312/413 5353
- Mon–Fri 10–4; Sun noon–5
- Blue line: UIC-Halsted
- 8
- Halsted
- Fair
- Free

The often-grim lot of impoverished immigrants to Chicago was made somewhat less miserable by the work of Jane Addams. In the late 19th century she created Hull House, a community and settlement centre in one of the city's most run-down neighbourhoods, and her efforts encouraged many of the US's earliest social reforms.

A better life Inspired by a visit to London's East End, Jane Addams founded Hull House in 1889, offering English-language and US citizenship courses, child care, music and art classes, and other services to the area's disparate ethnic groups – which included Germans, Irish, Poles, Ukrainians, Lithuanians and many more. She campaigned, with much success, for improved sanitation, the end of child labour, a minimum wage, improved working conditions in factories and for numerous other notable causes. With some 9,000 people using it each week at its peak, Hull House grew into a complex of 13 buildings. The two that remain sit elegantly, if incongruously, on the geometrically complex campus of the University of Illinois, most of which was designed by Walter Mesch of Skidmore, Owings & Merrill.

Prizewinning A 15-minute slide show tells the story of Addams and the settlement, while the rooms of the main building are lined by furnishings, letters, photos, awards and books from the house library (which began with Addams's old college books). These items chart the course of Hull House's growth, its vital role in Chicago, and the work that helped make Addams the most famous woman in America by the time she received the Nobel Peace Prize in 1931. The upper floor houses temporary exhibitions.

GRACELAND CEMETERY

Founded in 1860, Graceland is Chicago's most prestigious cemetery, the last resting place of many of the city's most influential people. Alongside great Chicagoans are a host of others, both famous and infamous.

Tombstone architecture Overlooked by high-rise lake-view apartments, its silence periodically broken by rumbling El trains, this is a very Chicago place to be buried. Even here, noted city architect Louis Sullivan leaves a mark with his elegant and ornate 1890 tomb for the steel magnate Henry Getty and his family. Sullivan himself is a Graceland resident, as are other Chicago architects such as Daniel Burnham, his partner, John Root, and international style guru Ludwig Mies van der Rohe. Railway-carriage manufacturer George Pullman has one of the largest tombs. Pullman died just three years after his workforce's bitter strike in 1894 (► 21), and his resting place was covered by tons of concrete to deter desecration.

Odd graves Among countless oddities to seek out (the free map issued from the office is an essential tool) are the baseball adorning the resting place of William A Hulbert (co-founder of the National League), and the unnerving statue, *Eternal Silence* by Laredo Taft, marking the tomb of hotel-owner Dexter Graves.

DID YOU KNOW?

Also at Graceland:
- Philip D Armour (meat-packing mogul)
- Marshall Field (department-store founder)
- Bob Fitzsimmons (boxer)
- Jack Johnson (boxer)
- John Kinzie (fur trapper, early settler)
- Victor Lawson (newspaper publisher)
- Cyrus H McCormick (farm-machinery millionaire)
- Potter Palmer (property tycoon)
- Bertha Palmer (wife of Potter, and society queen)

INFORMATION

- ✚ Off map to north
- ✉ 4001 N Clark Street
- ☎ 312/525 1105
- 🕐 Office: Mon–Sat 8:30–4. Gates open during daylight hours
- 🚇 Brown line: Irving Park. Red line: Sheridan
- 🚌 80
- ♿ Good
- 💲 Free
- ↔ Wrigley Field (► 28), Lincoln Park (► 29)
- ❓ Guided walking tours operated Aug–Sep by the Chicago Architecture Foundation (☎ 312/922 3432)

WRIGLEY FIELD

The days of successive World Series wins may be a distant memory, but the baseball of the Chicago Cubs and the defiantly unmodern form of their Wrigley Field stadium, with its ivy-covered brick outfield wall, is as much a part of Chicago as deep-dish pizza and the elevated railroad.

DID YOU KNOW?

- Original name: Weeghman Park
- Original capacity: 14,000
- Original building cost: $250,000
- First occupants: Chicago Whales
- First National League match: April 1916
- Renamed: Cubs Park, 1920
- Renamed again: Wrigley Field, after owner William Wrigley Jr, 1926
- Seating capacity: 38,765
- Nickname: 'the friendly confines'

INFORMATION

- ✚ Off map to north
- ✉ 1060 W Addison Street
- ☎ 312/404 2827
- 🕐 Matches: Apr–early Oct
- 🍴 Fast-food stands (£); three restaurants (£–£££)
- Ⓡ Red line: Addison
- 🚌 22, 152
- ♿ Good
- 🎟 Match admission moderate to expensive
- ↔ Graceland Cemetery (➤ 27)

Uncomfortable Wrigley Field provides the perfect setting for America's traditional pastime. Built in 1914, the stadium has steadily resisted Astroturf, and the game takes place on grass within an otherwise perfectly ordinary city neighbourhood, now known as Wrigleyville. Denied car-parking space, most spectators endure densely packed El trains to reach the venue. Seating on the eastern side of Wrigley Field is single-tier and unroofed, exposing fans to the vagaries of Chicago weather, which during the April to October season can encompass anything from snow to sunshine and 100°F temperatures.

Hallmarks of tradition Nearby residents can watch the game from their windows. Some convert their roof space to box-like seating and charge admission. Locals also rent out their driveways as car parks. Above the seats is the much-loved 1937 scoreboard on which the numbers are moved not by computer chips but by human hands. Floodlights did not appear until 1988, and only after a fierce campaign of resistance. Someone in a high place may have objected: the first night match had to be abandoned due to rain.

LINCOLN PARK

This 6-mile-long, 1,200-acre green belt between the city and Lake Michigan has beaches, a zoo, a conservatory, a feast of statuary and much more. The park attracts Chicagoans of all kinds, in both winter and summer.

Small beginnings Created from sand dunes, swamp and the former city cemetery, Lincoln Park was established by the 1870s after its zoo had been started with the gift of two swans from New York's Central Park. Evolving over a number of years through the contributions of various designers, it is now the oldest and most visited park in the United States. The 35-acre zoo houses lions, elephants, apes, polar bears and penguins in replicated habitats; close by, the Conservatory, built in 1891, encompasses four separate greenhouses. Invitingly warm on cool and breezy Chicago days, the greenhouses provide balmy controlled climates for dazzling tropical and subtropical blooms and seasonal displays.

Beaches and bodies Tennis and badminton courts, putting greens, and ponds navigable in rented paddleboats are dotted across the rest of the park, linked by walking, jogging and cycle tracks. Facing the lake are several small beaches, crowded on sunny weekends. At the south end of the park are the Chicago Historical Society (▶ 33), and the Couch Mausoleum, which holds a few of the 20,000 corpses once buried beneath the park's southernmost reaches.

HIGHLIGHTS

- Lincoln Park Zoo
- The Conservatory
- Bates Fountain (conservatory garden)
- The Standing Lincoln
- Couch Mausoleum
- Beaches

Abraham Lincoln's statue in Lincoln Park

INFORMATION

- ✚ G/H1/2/3 and off map
- ✉ North of North Avenue, lining Lake Michigan
- ☎ Conservatory: 312/742 7737. Zoo: 312/742 2000
- ◉ Visit during daylight only
- 🍽 Cafeteria (£) and Ice Cream Shoppe (£)
- Ⓡ Red line: Armitage. Brown line: Fullerton (for zoo)
- 🚌 76, 77, 145, 146, 147, 151, 156
- ♿ Good
- 🎟 Free (including zoo)
- ↔ Chicago Historical Society (▶ 33)

29

SEARS TOWER

Although it is no longer the world's tallest building, Sears Tower does rise higher than any other structure in this city of skyscrapers. In addition to the unique and stylish architecture, it has the highest man-made vantage point in the western hemisphere.

DID YOU KNOW?

- Height: 1,454ft
- Height including antenna towers: 1,707ft
- Weight: 222,500 tons
- Square feet of floor space: 4.5 million
- Miles of plumbing: 25,000
- Miles of electrical wiring: 20,000
- Miles of telephone cable: 43,000
- Elevator speed: up to 1,600ft per minute
- Number of windows: 16,100
- View from Skydeck in clear weather: 45–50 miles

INFORMATION

- ➕ G7
- ✉ 233 S Wacker Drive
- ☎ 312/875 9696
- 🕐 Skydeck: Mar–Sep daily 9AM–11PM. Oct–Feb daily 9AM–10PM. (May be closed in high winds)
- 🍴 Various restaurants and cafés (£–£££)
- Ⓜ Brown and Orange lines: Quincy
- 🚌 1, 60, 151, 156
- ♿ Excellent
- 👐 Moderate
- ↔ Chicago Board of Trade (► 31), The Rookery (► 32), Carson Pirie Scott & Co Store (► 34)

Built from tubes From 1974 to 1996, Sears Tower's 110 storeys and 1,454ft height made it the tallest building in the world, rising from the Loop with a distinctive profile of black aluminium and bronze-tinted glass. Working for the firm of Skidmore, Owings & Merrill, architect Bruce Graham designed a structure involving the use of nine 75sq-ft bundled tubes, which steadily decline in number as the building reaches upwards. Aside from increasing the colossal structure's strength, this technique also echoes the stepback New York skyscraper style of the late 1920s. Among the early tasks during the three-year construction was the creation of foundation supports capable of holding a 222,500-ton building. At the opposite end, the two rooftop antennae were added in 1982, increasing the building's total height by 253ft and serving 21 broadcasting organisations based inside the tower.

Seeing for miles Although the audio-visual presentation on Chicago at ground level is lacklustre, the 103rd-floor Skydeck is not. Accessible via a 70-second elevator ride, it reveals a tremendous panorama of Chicago and its surroundings. In each direction, a recorded commentary describes the view and landmark buildings, seen here as few of them were ever intended to be seen: from above. Sears, the retail company that commissioned the building, moved out in 1992. Note Alexander Calder's remarkable moving sculpture, *Universe*, in the lobby at the Wacker Drive entrance.

CHICAGO BOARD OF TRADE

An aluminium statue of Ceres, the Roman goddess of agriculture, looks down over the Loop's financial institutions from the top of the Chicago Board of Trade. Strikingly sited above La Salle Street, this building embodies what Chicago is about.

Order from chaos Founded in 1848, the Chicago Board of Trade (CBOT) brought order and organisation to the previously chaotic system of grain trading, ending widely fluctuating prices and creating a stable market for the farm produce of the Midwest. Since 1930, the CBOT has occupied this architecturally eyecatching building, richly endowed with art deco motifs and a profusion of polished marble and shiny chrome.

Speedy dealing Ideally, arrive in the fifth-floor visitors' gallery shortly before the 9:30AM commencement of trading, and acquaint yourself with the layout of the trading floor. Each of a series of octagonal open pits specialises in one commodity. Above the pits, the walls are lined by screens that flash the latest prices for wheat, corn, soya beans and other produce. As trading begins, each pit becomes a flurry of activity. Traders here move an estimated $13 trillion across the floor each year.

DID YOU KNOW?

- Architects: Holabird & Root (1930), Murphy/Jahn (1983)
- Number of storeys: 45
- Trading room height: six storeys
- Trading floor size: 51,000sq ft
- Miles of telephone cable: 10,000
- Price changes displayed per day: 90,000
- Contracts exchanged annually: 13–14 million
- Ceres: sculpted by John H Storrs
- Height of Ceres: 31ft
- Height of Ceres above ground: 609ft

INFORMATION

- ✚ G7
- ✉ 141 W Jackson Boulevard
- ☎ 312/435 3590
- 🕐 Visitor centre: Mon–Fri 9–1:15. Closed holidays
- 🍴 Various restaurants and cafés (£–£££)
- Ⓜ Brown or Orange lines: Quincy
- 🚌 1, 60, 151
- ♿ Good
- 🎫 Free
- ↔ Sears Tower (➤ 30), The Rookery (➤ 32), Carson Pirie Scott & Co Store (➤ 34)

Top: trading begins
Left: CBOT façade

THE ROOKERY

Designed by Daniel Burnham and John Wellborn Root in the 1880s, and later renovated by Frank Lloyd Wright, the Rookery is among Chicago's most admired and most influential landmark buildings.

Bird house After the Great Fire of 1871, birds took to roosting in the water-storage building that was temporarily City Hall; it was consequently nicknamed the Rookery. Public feeling dictated that the site's new building should formally have this name. Rising 11 storeys, it was among the tallest buildings in the world on completion and one of the most important early skyscrapers: its load-bearing brick and granite walls, decorated with Roman, Moorish and Venetian (and several rook) motifs, support iron-framed upper levels, a construction that made it possible to build higher than ever before.

Interior treasures The façade, however, is scant preparation for the interior. The inner court seems to rise forever and is bathed in incredible levels of natural light entering through a vast domed skylight. Imposing lamps hang above the floor, and Root's intricate ironwork decorates the stairways that climb up to a 360-degree balcony. The sense of space and brightness is increased by the white marble, introduced by Frank Lloyd Wright in 1905.

Top: spiral stairways
Right: the Rookery

CHICAGO HISTORICAL SOCIETY

Almost as old as the city itself, the Chicago Historical Society not only has a fine collection of artefacts from the city's own fascinating back pages but is one of the world's leading institutions for displaying and appraising US history in general.

Chicago collections The society occupies a Georgian-style brick building constructed in 1932, with a modern, glass-walled extension, just inside Lincoln Park, near the south-west entrance. Generations of Chicago schoolchildren have come here to learn about their city's history. From the Union Stockyards to the Chicago Bears, every major facet in Chicago's rise from swampland to metropolis is discussed and illustrated in these chronologically arranged galleries. A page from an 1833 *Daily News* debating the possible impact of the coming of railroads, the city's first locomotive, and a colourful array of vintage rail company posters, demonstrate the city's significance as a transport centre. A lively display describes the gangster era; elsewhere the Haymarket Riot and Pullman Strike are thoughtfully covered and placed in context as part of the growth of the city's blue-collar militancy. Other exhibits cogently outline the emergence of Chicago as a centre for architectural innovation.

The American Wing Alongside temporary shows, the society's American Wing holds two exhibitions that explore US history via informative texts and an excellent collection of period items. 'We The People' charts the growth of the US from the fight for, and acquisition of, independence, to the creation of the constitution and the settlement of the West. 'A House Divided' focuses on the North–South conflicts in the young nation, looking particularly at the issue of slavery and the run-up to the Civil War.

HIGHLIGHTS

- *The Railsplitter*, painting of Abraham Lincoln
- Civil War surrender table
- John Brown's bible
- Abraham Lincoln's death bed
- 1920s bootleg liquor still
- Mementoes from 1893 World's Fair
- Chicago's first fire engine
- Poignant Great Fire exhibits

INFORMATION

- G3
- 1601 N Clark Street
- 312/642 4600
- Mon–Sat 9:30–4:30; Sun noon–5
- Light fare at the Big Shoulders Café (££)
- Brown line: Sedgwick
- 11, 22, 36, 72, 151, 156
- Good
- Inexpensive; free Mon
- Lincoln Park (➤ 29), International Museum of Surgical Sciences (➤ 38)

33

CARSON PIRIE SCOTT & CO STORE

DID YOU KNOW?

- 1856 Louis Sullivan born in Boston
- 1871–4 Studies architecture at Massachusetts Institute of Technology and at École de Beaux-Arts in Paris
- 1875 Moves to Chicago
- 1881 Forms architectural practice of Adler & Sullivan with Dankmar Adler
- 1886 Commences building of Chicago's acclaimed Auditorium Building
- 1890 Completes Getty tomb for Graceland Cemetery
- 1924 *Autobiography of an Idea* is published; it includes Sullivan's phrase 'form follows function'. In the same year, Sullivan dies impoverished

INFORMATION

- ✚ H6
- ✉ 1 S State Street
- ☎ 312/641 7000
- ◉ Tue–Wed, Fri–Sat 9:45–5:45; Mon and Thu 9:45–7:30
- Ⓜ Blue line: Madison. Red line: Monroe
- 🚌 22, 23, 36, 56, 157
- ♿ Good
- 🎫 Free
- ↔ Sears Tower (➤ 30), Chicago Board of Trade (➤ 31), The Rookery (➤ 32), Chicago Cultural Center (➤ 37), Art Institute of Chicago (➤ 40), Grant Park (➤ 41)

Probably no other store in the world can claim a more elaborately decorated exterior than that of Carson Pirie Scott & Co, created by the phenomenally gifted and influential architect Louis Sullivan over a five-year period from 1899.

Nature's art While Sullivan was a key figure in what became known as the Chicago School of Architecture – the group that, after Chicago's Great Fire, gave the city the earliest skyscrapers – it was for his finely realised ornamentation that he became best known. With the Carson Pirie Scott & Co Store, Sullivan's predilection for flowing yet geometric forms created in cast iron reached new levels of artistry. Nowhere are his skills better expressed than in the store's corner entrance on State and Madison streets, and around the store's first- and second-floor windows, the showpiece windows intended to display merchandise.

Light and space The more austere terracotta-clad upper levels express the steel form of the building. The large windows span the entire width between the steel supports: known as 'Chicago windows', and made possible by the invention of plate glass, they accentuate the horizontal, maximise the amount of natural light reaching the interior, and strengthen the general sense of geometric cohesion. A 1979 renovation restored many of Sullivan's forgotten features.

12

WRIGLEY BUILDING

In a prime site on classy Michigan Avenue stands the 1920s Wrigley Building, an elegant monument to high-rise architecture and to the Chicago-based company that is still the world's major manufacturer of chewing-gum.

Forever gleaming The Wrigley Building was partly modelled on the Giralda Tower in Seville, Spain, although the many ornamental features echo the French Renaissance. It is actually two buildings rather than one. The North and South buildings stand behind a continuous façade linked by an arcaded walkway at ground level and by two enclosed aerial walkways. The ornate glazed terracotta façade has never been restored but has kept its original gleam. The effect is most pronounced at night when the exterior is illuminated by banks of 1,000-watt bulbs.

Northern pioneer It is hard to believe today, but at the time of the Wrigley Building's construction there were no office buildings north of the Loop. It was raised at the same time as the Michigan Avenue Bridge, and was always intended to be the gateway to the city's so-called Near North neighbourhoods. The building's offices were fully rented soon after completion, and house public relations, advertising and publishing companies.

DID YOU KNOW?

- Architects: Graham, Anderson, Probst & White
- Excavation begins: Jan 1920
- Completion: South Building – April 1921; North Building – May 1924
- Height: 425ft
- Storeys: South – 30; North – 21
- Area: 453,433sq ft
- Office workers employed in building: 1,300
- Clock-face diameter: 19ft 7in
- Clock hour-hand length: 6ft 4in
- Clock minute-hand length: 9ft 2in

INFORMATION

- ✚ H5
- ✉ 400 N Michigan Avenue
- ☎ 312/923 8080
- 🕐 Usual business hours
- Ⓠ Red line: Grand
- 🚌 3, 11, 29, 65, 147, 151, 157
- ♿ Good
- 🆓 Free
- ↔ Terra Museum of American Art (► 36), Tribune Tower (► 39), Glessner House Museum (► 43), Museum of Contemporary Art (► 52), IBM Building (► 55)

35

13

TERRA MUSEUM OF AMERICAN ART

HIGHLIGHTS

- *The Jolly Flatboatman*, George Caleb Bingham
- *The Last of the Mohicans*, Thomas Cole
- *Our Banner in the Sky*, Frederick Church
- *The Checker Players*, Milton Avery
- *Brooklyn Bridge on the River*, Max Weber

INFORMATION

- H5
- 666 N Michigan Avenue
- 312/664 3939
- Tue noon–8; Wed–Sat 10–5; Sun noon–5
- None
- Red line: Grand
- 3, 11, 125, 145, 146, 147, 151
- Moderate donation requested; free Tue and first Sun of month
- Wrigley Building (➤ 35), Tribune Tower (➤ 39), Museum of Contemporary Art (➤ 52), IBM Building (➤ 55)
- Free guided tours: Tue–Sun noon and 2

Top: The Last of the Mohicans *by Thomas Cole (1801–48)*

With both temporary and long-term exhibitions of quality, the Terra Museum insightfully explores the development of art in the US and the rise to international pre-eminence of some of the nation's artists.

Industrial art The Terra is a rarity among the nation's art museums in having been designed solely to display American art. The museum was founded by wealthy industrialist-entrepreneur Daniel J Terra – who built a fortune on fast-drying ink – to showcase his own collections. The museum also borrows works for the frequently outstanding temporary shows that highlight work by American artists who have been neglected or otherwise undervalued by mainstream art museums. Terra, who served as a cultural affairs ambassador in the Reagan administration, also opened a sister museum in Giverney, France, to display American works painted in that country. Inspired by New York's Guggenheim, the Terra's design includes ramps between floors so that you can start at the top level and wind your way down.

The galleries Following several Whistler etchings, the 'Attitudes Towards Nature' gallery explores the changing face of the American landscape as depicted by its early painters, among them Thomas Cole (founder of the Hudson River School), Thomas Moran and Frederick Church. Subsequent rooms display works by important figures such as William Homer and George Caleb Bingham, and lead into walls of moderns, including pieces by Joseph Stella, Edward Hopper and Milton Avery. A well-lit alcove is the setting for the 'collection cameo', where a particular work is hung alongside a detailed accompanying text.

CHICAGO CULTURAL CENTER

Even in a city so richly endowed with architectural marvels, the stunning, turn-of-the-century Chicago Cultural Center – nicknamed 'the people's palace' – is a treasure. It hosts scores of free exhibitions, and it is the permanent home of the Museum of Broadcast Communications.

The exhibitions Completed in 1897 and serving as the city's main public library until 1974, the Chicago Cultural Center mounts displays that usually focus on aspects of Chicago history and architecture. Several exhibitions run concurrently. The entertaining Museum of Broadcast Communications explores the history of US radio and TV with displays of vintage transmitting and receiving equipment, and recordings of historic broadcasts. Much more impressive to first-time visitors is the sheer grandeur of the building, with its gleaming marble, stained glass and polished brass, all in *beaux-arts* style.

The architecture The Washington Street entrance leads visitors through hefty bronze doors set beneath a Romanesque portal into the main lobby, where the grand staircase is bordered by exquisite mosaics set into its white Carrara marble balustrades. A visitor information office occupies part of the second floor, while the third holds the Preston Bradley Hall, whose awe-inspiring 38ft Tiffany-glass dome has been valued at $35 million. The main exhibition hall is on the next level, where gorgeously decorated columns rise to an immaculately coffered ceiling.

DID YOU KNOW?

- Architects: Holabird & Root (1897)
- Restoration: Shepley, Rutan & Coolridge (1977, 1993)
- Main exhibition space area: 7,600ft
- Number of exhibition visitors: 600,000 annually

INFORMATION

- ➕ H6
- ✉ 78 E Washington Street
- ☎ 312/346 3278
- 🕐 Mon–Fri 10–6; Sat 10–5; Sun noon–5
- 🍴 Good café (£)
- Ⓜ Brown and Orange lines: Madison
- 🚌 3, 4, 60, 145, 147, 151
- ♿ Good
- 🎫 Free
- ↔ Carson Pirie Scott & Co Store (➤ 34), Art Institute of Chicago (➤ 40), Grant Park (➤ 41)
- ❓ Guided architectural tours: Tue, Wed and Sat (☎ 312/744 6630)

15

MUSEUM OF SURGICAL SCIENCES

HIGHLIGHTS

- *Professor W T Eckley's Dissecting Class (photo)*
- *Trepanned Peruvian skulls*
- *15th–16th-century amputation saw*
- *Needles and probes from Pompeii*
- *1950s X-ray shoe-fitter*
- *Gallstone collection*
- *Civil War field amputation kit*
- *Reprint of Versalius's notebook*
- *Laennec's stethoscope*

INFORMATION

- ✚ H3
- ✉ 1524 N Lake Shore Drive
- ☎ 312/642 6502
- 🕐 Tue–Sat 10–4; Sun 11–5
- 🚇 Brown line: Sedgwick
- 🚌 151
- ♿ Good
- 💲 Free; donation suggested
- ↔ Lincoln Park (▶ 29), Chicago Historical Society (▶ 33)

Ancient surgery: a drilled skull

When Peruvian surgeons drilled into their patients' skulls 2,000 years ago, they probably never imagined that their handiwork would eventually be displayed in the International Museum of Surgical Sciences, which traces medical advances and surgical skills through the ages.

House of health Founded in 1953, the museum is dedicated to enhancing the understanding of surgery past and present. It has several floors of exhibits, as well as innovative temporary shows covering diverse subjects related to health and medicine. The collection is housed in a stately mansion designed by celebrated Chicago architect Howard Van Doren Shaw and completed in 1917. A visit here not only informs on surgical matters but provides an insight into the domestic arrangements of a moneyed Chicago family of the early 20th century.

Tools of the trade Among the oldest exhibits are drilled skulls discovered in ancient Peruvian temples, surgeons' tools found in excavations at the Roman town of Pompeii, and ancestor skulls used by shamans of Papua New Guinea to frighten evil spirits. Pioneering surgeons from various countries are commemorated with somber portraits and, in one case, a bronze replica of the surgeon's right hand. Many rooms are

packed with displays of fearsome needles, hooks, and other sharp metallic things used for all manner of gouging, probing and extracting. Less unnerving are the early microscopes, the room filled with bulky X-ray machines, and the stethoscope of one Doctor Theophile Laennec, which was designed to be fitted inside a top hat.

TRIBUNE TOWER

In the 1920s, the **Chicago Tribune** *newspaper staged a competition for the design of its new premises. The competition attracted many leading architects, and the winning entry has become one of the most loved elements of this fashionable stretch of Michigan Avenue.*

Modern medieval Although Eliel Saarinen's second-placed entry came to wield greater influence on the future of high-rise building, it was the Gothic-influenced design by John Mead Howells and Raymond Hood that took the $100,000 first prize. Using vertical lines of differing width and a buttressed tower, Howells and Hood created a 46-storey building that looks like an elongated medieval cathedral. The structure was completed in 1925.

Stone-studded The building is best admired from a distance, although the lobby displays two former *Tribune* front pages, one marking the Great Fire of 1871 and the other America's entry into World War I. WGN, the Tribune-owned radio station, can be watched through its studio's ground-level window. Embedded in the building's walls are stones from the world's most famous landmark buildings, pilfered by *Tribune* foreign correspondents at the request of Robert McCormick, the paper's larger-than-life publisher for 45 years, from 1910 until his death in 1955.

DID YOU KNOW?

Tribune Tower includes stones from:
● The Berlin Wall, Germany
● The Alamo, Texas
● The Great Wall, China
● Westminster Abbey, London
● Notre Dame, Paris
● The Great Pyramid, Egypt
● St Peter's, Rome
● The Colosseum, Rome
● Hans Christian Andersen's home, Denmark

INFORMATION

✚ H5
✉ 435 N Michigan Avenue
☎ 312/222 3994
⏲ Normal business hours
Ⓜ Red line: Grand
🚌 3, 11, 29, 65, 147, 151, 157
♿ Good
💲 Free
↔ Wrigley Building (➤ 35), Terra Museum of American Art (➤ 36), Glessner House Museum (➤ 43), Museum of Contemporary Art (➤ 52), IBM Building (➤ 55)

Top: a radio show in progress
Left: the Tribune Tower entrance

17

ART INSTITUTE OF CHICAGO

HIGHLIGHTS

- *Time Transfixed*, Magritte
- *Personages with Stars*, Miró
- *Improvisation 30 (Cannons)*, Kandinsky
- *Mother and Child*, Picasso
- *Two Sisters (on the Terrace)*, Renoir
- *Bedroom at Arles*, Van Gogh
- The Arthur Rubloff Paperweight Collection

INFORMATION

- ✚ H7
- ✉ 111 S Michigan Avenue
- ☎ 312/443 3600
- 🕐 Mon, Wed–Fri 10:30–4:30; Tue 10:30–8; Sat 10–5; Sun noon–5
- 🍴 £–£££
- Ⓜ Brown and Orange lines: Adams
- 🚌 3, 4, 60, 145, 147, 151
- ♿ Good
- 🎫 Moderate; free on Tue
- 🔗 Carson Pirie Scott & Co Store (➤ 34), Chicago Cultural Center (➤ 37), Grant Park (➤ 41)
- ❓ Free tours daily

In a classically inspired building erected for the World's Columbian Exposition (1893), the Art Institute of Chicago has an acclaimed collection of Impressionist paintings, but its spacious galleries showcase much more, from arms and armour to the original trading room of the Stock Exchange.

Masterworks Except for the celebrated *American Gothic* by Grant Wood, which is displayed amid the American collections, the pick of the paintings is the European art grouped chronologically around the second floor. No work receives greater notice and admiration than Seurat's expansive *A Sunday Afternoon on the Island of La Grande Jatte*, a pointillist masterpiece. Seminal works in adjacent galleries include haystacks by Monet, dancers by Degas, a self-portrait on cardboard by Van Gogh, and the vibrant *Paris Street, Rainy Day* by the less well-known Gustave Caillebotte. Among the many striking modern works are Picasso's *The Old Guitarist* and Hopper's moody *Nighthawks*.

Curiosities Everything from Chinese ceramics to Guatemalan textiles has a niche on the first floor. There is a huge collection of paperweights, and there are swords, daggers and chainmail – but leave time for the stunning 1898 Trading Room of the Chicago Stock Exchange, designed by Louis Sullivan and reconstructed here.

Above: Grant Wood's American Gothic

GRANT PARK

Planned by Daniel Burnham in 1909 as the centrepiece of a series of lakefront parks to beautify the fast-growing metropolis, Grant Park is a major festival venue that in its past has seen everything from an infamous violence-marred 1968 anti-Vietnam War demonstration to the Pope leading mass in 1979.

City views Far from being the bucolic extravagance visitors might expect, Grant Park is essentially a succession of lawns criss-crossed by walkways and split in two by the busy Lake Shore Drive. Bordered by the high-rises of the Loop and the expanses of Lake Michigan, Grant Park never lets you forget that you are in Chicago. It provides a hospitable setting for summer concerts at the Petrillo Music Shell, and other events.

Buildings banished A section of today's park was designated as public land in 1836, but it reached its present size by expanding on to rubble from the 1871 fire, dumped as landfill in Lake Michigan. Its prime commercial location made Grant Park a target for developers, and only the energy and finances of Chicago-based mail-order pioneer A Montgomery Ward, who engaged in a series of court battles, kept buildings from going up on its 319 acres. Among the features is the 1926 Buckingham Fountain, notable for its computer-choreographed display of coloured lights dancing on the 1.5 million gallons of water that are pumped daily.

Events Grant Park is the venue for the city's most popular annual open-air events, including blues, jazz and gospel music festivals, classical music in the Petrillo Music Shell, and the well-attended Taste of Chicago.

HIGHLIGHTS

- Blues Festival (June)
- Gospel Festival (June)
- Taste of Chicago (June–July)
- Independence Day concert and firework display (July)
- Jazz Festival (September)

INFORMATION

- ✚ H/J6/7/8/9
- ✉ Bordered by N Michigan Avenue, E Randolph Drive, Roosevelt Drive and Lake Michigan
- ☎ Petrillo Music Shell concert information: 312/819 0614
- 🕐 Visit during daylight hours only, except for special evening events
- 🚇 Brown and Orange lines: Randolph, Madison, Adams
- 🚌 3, 4, 6, 38, 60, 145, 146, 147, 151, 157
- ♿ Good
- 🎫 Free
- ↔ Carson Pirie Scott & Co Store (➤ 34), Chicago Cultural Center (➤ 37), Art Institute of Chicago (➤ 40), Field Museum of Natural History (➤ 42), John G Shedd Aquarium (➤ 44), Adler Planetarium & Astronomy Museum (➤ 46)

19

FIELD MUSEUM OF NATURAL HISTORY

HIGHLIGHTS

- 'DNA to Dinosaurs'
- 'Travelling the Pacific'
- Egyptian tomb
- Gem collection
- Pawnee earth lodge
- Tibet collections

INFORMATION

- H/J8
- E Roosevelt Road at Lake Shore Drive
- 312/922 9410
- Daily 9–5
- Coffee shop (£); McDonald's (£)
- Orange line: Roosevelt
- 146
- Roosevelt Road
- Good
- Moderate; free Wed
- Grant Park (➤ 41), John G Shedd Aquarium (➤ 44), Adler Planetarium (➤ 46)

An impressive exhibit in the dinosaur section

There are few better places in Chicago than the Field Museum of Natural History to entertain and educate young minds, though adults will also find much to amuse and inform among displays drawn from all corners of the globe. After a strenuous round of viewing, ponder the fact that only around one per cent of the museum's 20 million artefacts is on display.

The building The museum was completed in 1920, its cavernous galleries providing a home for a collection originally assembled for Chicago's 1893 World's Columbian Exposition. With its porticoes, columns and *beaux-arts* decoration, the imposing design sits rather uneasily with the needs of a modern museum, and sometimes the many rooms of exhibits from myriad eras and cultures make for difficult viewing. None the less, steady upgrading and innovative ideas in layout make certain parts a rip-roaring success.

Great exhibits The outstanding sections include: the 'DNA to Dinosaurs' exhibit, which uses multimedia techniques to explore 3.8 billion years of evolution; the ancient Egyptian artefacts (5000 BC to AD 300), arranged in and around the innards of a life-size re-created 5th-dynasty pharaoh's tomb; and 'Travelling the Pacific', an examination of cultural and spiritual life in the Pacific and the threats posed by the Western world's encroachment. Also noteworthy are the Native American displays and the gem collection, which includes pieces purchased in the 1890s from the famous Tiffany & Co jewellers.

GLESSNER HOUSE MUSEUM

Perhaps only in Chicago could a farm-machinery mogul build a home that would profoundly influence American domestic architecture and inspire future designers such as Louis Sullivan. Simply put, the Glessner House is a beautiful house and still in beautiful shape.

Outside In 1885 a leading Chicago couple, John and Frances Glessner, commissioned Boston architect Henry Hobson Richardson to design a home for them. The Glessners' house is the only surviving example of Richardson's work. In contrast to the European revival-style homes dominating what was then Chicago's most fashionable neighbourhood, the Glessners' house was given a fortress-like stone-wall façade, and an L-shape that enabled its main rooms to face not the streets, as was the vogue, but an inner coutyard. Initially, neighbours found the house objectionable, but many revised their opinions once invited in.

Inside As you enter the house, oak beams and panels exude an immediate warmth, and clever planning has created subtle distinctions between public areas (for entertaining) and private ones. Many furnishings were designed by Hobson, including the large oak desk in the library which, significantly for the time, was intended as a workplace for Mrs Glessner as well as for her husband. The Glessners' own appreciation of art and design is reflected in their use of William Morris tiles and wall coverings, and the Isaac Scott ceramics and cabinets. John Glessner's photographs – on display in the house – confirm that the present-day appearance of the house and its furnishings is much the same as that enjoyed by the Glessners until their deaths in the 1930s.

DID YOU KNOW

- 1838 Henry Hobson Richardson born in Louisiana
- 1859 Graduates from Harvard and becomes the second American to study at the École de Beaux-Arts in Paris
- 1873 Establishes a reputation with the Romanesque-style church in Boston
- 1885 Construction of the Marshall Field Wholesale Warehouse begins, filling a city block and heightening Richardson's renown in Chicago
- 1886 Dies just prior to the completion of the Glessner House

INFORMATION

- H9
- 1800 S Prairie Avenue
- 312/326 1480
- Guided tours: Wed–Sun 1, 2, 3
- Red line: Cermak/Chinatown
- 1, 18, 38
- Few
- Moderate
- Clarke House (➤ 54)

21

JOHN G SHEDD AQUARIUM

HIGHLIGHTS

- Pacific white-sided dolphins
- Beluga whales
- Sea otters
- Sea anemones
- Penguins
- Turtles

INFORMATION

- ⊞ J8
- ✉ 1200 S Lake Shore Drive
- ☎ 312/939 2426
- 🕐 Memorial Day–Labor Day daily 9–6. Rest of year Mon–Fri 9–5; Sat–Sun 9–6
- 🍽 Soundings Restaurant (££); snacks from various stands at Bubble Net Food Court (£)
- Ⓜ Orange line: Roosevelt
- 🚌 146
- 🚉 Roosevelt Road
- ♿ Excellent
- 💲 Moderate. Thu: aquarium free; other exhibits reduced fee
- ↔ Grant Park (➤ 41), Field Museum (➤ 42), Adler Planetarium (➤ 46)

Chicago's 'Ocean-by-the-Lake' is the world's largest indoor aquarium, greatly enhanced by the addition of a state-of-the-art oceanarium.

Aquarium A re-created Caribbean coral reef at the centre of this imposing Greek-style building is home to barracuda, moray eels, nurse sharks and other creatures fed several times daily by a team of microphone-equipped divers, who describe the creatures, their habits and their habitat as they hand them their dinner. Around the reef, denizens of the deep waters of the world occupy geographically arranged tanks. Look for the false-eye flashlight fish, born with the piscine equivalent of a torch; the mimic roundhead, able to deter predators by making its lower half resemble a moray eel; and the matamata turtle, so sluggish that you'll be lucky to see it move.

Oceanarium Dolphins and whales are the star attractions here. Five times daily, the dolphins and their human trainers display some of the animals' natural skills (such as 'spy-hopping', when a dolphin raises itself onto its tail) to an audience seated around a re-created chunk of Pacific Northwest coast. Winding nature trails

lead to the lower floors and to windows that provide an underwater view of the dolphins and whales; a colony of penguins; and hands-on exhibits that describe facets of sea-mammal life, such as underwater movement, respiratory system, diet, mating habits, and interaction with other sea creatures.

Decorations on the aquarium door illustrate the sea life within

DU SABLE MUSEUM

One of the unsung museums of Chicago, the Du Sable Museum of African-American History chronicles aspects of black history, focusing chiefly on African-Americans but also encompassing the cultures of Africa and the Caribbean.

South Side settlers The museum is named after Chicago's first permanent settler, Jean-Baptiste Point du Sable (a Haitian trader born of a French father and African slave mother). Subsequent African-American arrivals came in three main waves – during the late 19th century and during the two World Wars – settling mostly on Chicago's South Side. Black businesses became established, and the expanding community provided the voter base

Part of the display of African sculpture

for the first blacks to enter Chicago politics. Among the settlers were many musicians, and what became Chicago blues was born – an electrified urban form of rural blues fused with elements of jazz. The turbulent 1960s saw growing radicalism among Chicago's African-Americans, and the start of the rise to national prominence of South Side's Jesse Jackson.

Exhibits The ground-floor rooms display items from the permanent collection, but there are also meticulously planned temporary exhibitions which in the past have featured the sacred art of Ethiopia, and celebrated the life and music of Duke Ellington.

DID YOU KNOW?

- 1850 Passing of Illinois' Fugitive Slave Law makes Chicago an important stop on the 'Underground Railroad' of escaped slaves
- 1871 First Chicago black elected to public office
- 1900 Chicago's black population: 31,150
- 1905 Founding of the nationally influential African-American-run newspaper, *Chicago Defender*
- 1919 What newspapers call a 'race riot' leaves 38 dead
- 1940 Chicago's black population: 278,000
- 1950 Chicago's black population: 492,000
- 1968 Jesse Jackson founds PUSH on South Side
- 1983 Harold Washington is elected Chicago's first black mayor

INFORMATION

- ✚ Off map to south
- ✉ 740 E 56th Place
- ☎ 773/947 0600
- ◷ Mon–Fri 9–5; Sat–Sun noon–5
- Ⓡ Red line: Garfield
- ▤ 4
- ▣ 59th Street
- ♿ Good
- ▯ Moderate; free on Thu
- ⟷ Oriental Institute (➤ 47), Museum of Science and Industry (➤ 48)

23

ADLER PLANETARIUM

Bringing close-up views of deep space to Chicagoans and other earthlings, the Friday evening Sky Show has helped the Adler Planetarium and Astronomy Museum to win a place in local hearts.

HIGHLIGHTS

- Sky Show
- Apache Point Observing Station link-up
- Space Transporters
- Martian rocks
- Voyager images of Saturn

INFORMATION

- ✚ J8
- ✉ 1300 S Lake Shore Drive
- ☎ 312/322 0304
- 🕐 June–Labor Day Mon–Wed 9–5; Thu–Fri 9–9; Sat–Sun 9–6. Rest of year Mon–Thu 9–5; Fri 9–9; Sat–Sun 9–6
- 🍴 Simple cafeteria (£)
- Ⓜ Orange line: Roosevelt
- 🚌 146
- 🚏 Roosevelt Road
- ♿ Good
- 🎟 Moderate; free entry to building on Tue
- ↔ Grant Park (➤ 41), Field Museum of Natural History (➤ 42), John G Shedd Aquarium (➤ 44)

Skywatching Max Adler, a Sears Roebuck executive, realised his ambition to put the wonders of the cosmos within the reach of ordinary people when he provided the money to have the western hemisphere's first modern planetarium built in Chicago. Opened in 1930, the planetarium's floors, corridors and stairways hold one of the world's major astronomical collections. The landmark building is a dodecahedron in rainbow granite, decorated by signs of the zodiac and topped by a lead-covered copper dome. The hour-long Sky Show examines themes in astronomy, first using a multimedia theatre and then the 68ft dome of the Sky Theater. On Friday evenings the Sky Show displays live images from the observatory's own 20in computer-controlled telescope.

Finding space The museum's collections are thematically arranged on three floors linked by stairways showing deep-space photographs. An extraordinary collection of astrolabes and other

items portrays the astronomy of the Middle Ages. Navigation and the development of telescopes are the main theme on the second floor, where pride of place goes to the exhibit on Sir William Herschel, the musician-turned-astronomer who discovered Uranus in 1781. The first floor gets to grips with space exploration, displaying an Apollo space suit and samples of Martian rock.

ORIENTAL INSTITUTE

The Oriental Institute, on the University of Chicago campus, is one of the leading museums and research centres specialising in the Middle East, and the sheer volume of exhibits alone creates a powerful impression of ancient cultures.

The history In the 1890s, the newly founded University of Chicago was already showing off a modest collection of Middle East antiquities. As the university embarked on its own field trips the collections expanded significantly, and in 1919 the Oriental Institute was established. Since then, the institute's finds, and its acclaimed interpretation of them, have greatly enhanced the understanding and appreciation of the once mighty kingdoms of Egypt, Assyria, Anatolia, Mesopotamia and neighbouring regions. The museum was purpose-built in 1931 by the firm of Mayers, Murray & Phillips, who included numerous Middle Eastern architectural motifs. A major renovation during the 1990s restored many of the original features.

The galleries Amid the mummy masks, royal seals and polished clay pots, several sizeable pieces particularly stand out. Dominating the Egyptian section is an enormous statue of Tutankhamun, from his tomb in the Valley of Kings. In the Assyrian section is the human-headed winged bull, an immense sculpture that once stood in the palace of the powerful Sargon II (reigned 721–705 BC). Also from Sargon II's palace is a stone relief, showing two officials. The museum's whole collection – so extensive that only a small fraction can be displayed at one time – spans about 3,000 years, from the 2nd millennium BC.

HIGHLIGHTS

- Tutankhamun statue
- Human-headed winged bull
- Relief from the tomb of Mentuemhat
- Striding lion
- Clay prism of Sennacherib
- Egyptian Book of the Dead
- Archaic-period bed
- Statue of Horus
- Mesopotamian four-faced god and goddess

INFORMATION

- ✚ Off map to south
- ✉ 1155 East 58th Street
- ☎ 312/702 1062
- 🕐 Tue, Thu–Sat 10–4; Wed 10–8:30; Sun noon–4
- Ⓡ Red line: Garfield
- 🚌 4, 55
- 🚉 59th Street
- ♿ Good
- 🎟 Free
- ↔ Du Sable Museum of African-American History (➤ 45), Museum of Science and Industry (➤ 48)

Top: Sumerian votive statues
Left: a sandstone statue of Tutankhamun

MUSEUM OF SCIENCE & INDUSTRY

HIGHLIGHTS

- AIDS exhibit
- 'Take Flight'
- Apollo 8
- Space Shuttle
- Simulated F14 mission
- Piccard Stratosphere Glider
- Re-created coal mine
- Heart
- 'Managing Urban Wastes' exhibit

INFORMATION

- ✚ Off map to south
- ✉ 57th Street at Lake Shore Drive
- ☎ 773/684 1414
- 🕐 Summer daily 9:30–5:30. Rest of the year Mon–Fri 9:30–4; Sat–Sun 9:30–5:30
- 🍴 Several cafés (£)
- Ⓜ Red line: Garfield
- 🚌 6, 10
- 🚉 55th, 56th, 57th Street
- ♿ Excellent
- 💰 Moderate; free on Thu; separate charge for Omnimax Theater
- ↔ Du Sable Museum of African-American History (▶ 45), Oriental Institute (▶ 47)

With 2,000 exhibits spread across 15 acres, the Museum of Science and Industry easily fills a day. Even know–it–all visitors find hours passing like minutes as they discover new things about the world – and beyond it – at every turn.

Flying high The first eye-catching item is a Boeing 727 attached to an interior balcony. Packed with multimedia exhibits, the plane simulates a flight from San Francisco to Chicago, making full use of flaps, rudders and undercarriage, all fully explained. Other flight-related exhibits include a simulated mission aboard a naval F-14 fighter. Reflecting other modes of transport are the 500mph Spirit of America car, a walk through a 1944 German U-boat, and the Apollo 8 spacecraft. The moon-circling Apollo craft forms just a small part of the excellent Henry Crown Space Center, housed in an adjoining building.

Medical matters A 16ft-high walk-through heart sits among exhibits detailing the workings of the human body. Close by, in the AIDS exhibit, imaginative devices explain much about viruses and the immune system. The display includes a computer-generated voyage into the body, which illustrates the attack strategy of the HIV virus and the various approaches being used by scientists to combat it.

CHICAGO's *best*

NEIGHBOURHOODS

CHINATOWN

Other Chinese enclaves exist in Chicago but the longest-established area of Cantonese settlement – and what the city thinks of as Chinatown – is the eight blocks around the junction of Wentworth Avenue and Cermak Road, south of the city centre. Packed with restaurants and bakeries, herbalists and tea shops, Chinatown resounds to the snap of firecrackers each January or February during Chinese New Year, one of Chicago's liveliest festivals.

One of many busy restaurants in Chinatown

⊞ G9/10 🚇 Red line: Cermak/Chinatown 🚌 24

HYDE PARK AND KENWOOD

Between Hyde Park Boulevard and the University of Chicago campus, Hyde Park became established, from the 1880s, as a leafy suburb complete with two parks designed by Olmsted and Vaux. Many early homes have been demolished, but some remain in Kenwood, north of Hyde Park Boulevard. Both neighbourhoods are now predominantly populated by liberal professionals, and have numerous bookshops and restaurants.

⊞ Off map 🚇 Red line: Garfield 🚌 1, 4, 28, 51 🚉 Hyde Park-53rd

The Gold Coast

In the late 19th century, a top Chicago businessman astonished his peers by erecting a mansion home on undeveloped land well north of the Loop close to Lake Michigan. As others followed, the area became known as the Gold Coast (⊞ H3/4), its streets lined by the elegant townhouses of the city's great and good. Many of the homes remain, joined by ultra-luxurious apartment towers.

THE LOOP

So-named for its position within the loop formed by the El (elevated railway), the Loop is Chicago's business district and the home of the city's most celebrated architecture. The Loop is the vibrant hub of the city by day – virtually deserted by night.

⊞ G/H6/7 🚇 All El lines converge on the Loop 🚌 Most north–south routes

MAGNIFICENT MILE

The section of Michigan Avenue between the Chicago River and Oak Street was named the Magnificent Mile by a property developer in the 1940s. The favoured shopping strip for wealthy Chicagoans, its elegant shops, gleaming high-rise shopping malls and designer outlets pay some of the city's highest commercial rents.

✚ H4/5 🚇 Red line: Grand, Chicago 🚌 3, 11, 125, 145, 146, 147, 151

OAK PARK

From 1889, Frank Lloyd Wright added some 25 buildings in his evolving Prairie School style to the more orthodox Victorian homes along Oak Park's tree-lined streets, 8 miles west of the Loop. Ernest Hemingway (➤ 53) called the area a town of 'broad lawns and narrow minds'.

✚ Off map to west 🚇 Metra Line West 🚌 23 🚇 Oak Park

A book market in full swing in Printer's Row

PRINTER'S ROW

The industrial buildings lining Dearborn Street, which runs south from the Loop, were the centre of Chicago's printing industry during the late 19th century. Many are now loft-style apartments, with galleries and restaurants at street level.

✚ G7 🚇 Blue line: La Salle. Red line: Harrison 🚌 22, 62

RIVER NORTH

In the angle formed by the two branches of the Chicago River north of the Loop, commercial art galleries, auction houses, eateries and nightspots now fill the handsome old warehouses.

✚ G/H5/6 🚇 Brown line: Chicago. Red line: Grand, Chicago 🚌 22, 37, 41, 65, 66

UKRAINIAN VILLAGE

Ukrainians settled this area off W Chicago Avenue during the early 1900s. Evidence of the old country includes St Nicholas Cathedral (➤ 56), Ukrainian eateries and shops, a culture centre, and Ukrainian Independence Day festivities on 22 January.

✚ C5 🚇 Blue line: Chicago 🚌 66

Wicker Park and Bucktown

The 4-acre park on Damen Avenue that gives Wicker Park (✚ C/D3/4) its name is enclosed by grey-stone mansions. These days Wicker Park and neighbouring Bucktown (north of Milwaukee Avenue) are fashionably bohemian and known for their alternative music clubs and coffee bars, which regularly stage poetry readings and performance art events.

A Printer's Row mural illustrates the area's past

MUSEUMS

American Police Center & Museum

Grainy photos of Chicago cops through the decades and displays on the 1886 Haymarket Riot and the 1968 Democratic Convention are among the exhibits at this barn-like museum (✉ 1717 S State Street). Other sections detail Chigaco's gangster era and the capture in the city of John Dillinger. A wooden electric chair, believed to have been used during the 1920s, is also on view.

BALZEKAS MUSEUM OF LITHUANIAN CULTURE

Regional folk costumes and other Lithuanian historical items form part of an extensive and absorbing collection.

➕ Off map ✉ 6500 S Pulaski Road ☎ 773/582 6500 🕐 Daily 10–4 🚇 Orange line: Midway 🚌 53A 🚻 Few 💰 Moderate

Display of textiles in the Balzekas Museum of Lithuanian Culture

MUSEUM OF CONTEMPORARY ART

Highlights from the permanent collection include the works of the Chicago-based Ed Paschke, and Richard Long's *Chicago Mud Circle* (1996), created directly on to a gallery wall. The lower levels house temporary exhibitions and provide access to the Sculpture Garden.

➕ H5 ✉ 220 E Chicago Avenue ☎ 312/280 5161 or 312/280 2660 🕐 Tue, Thu–Fri 11–6; Wed 11–9; Sat–Sun 10–6 🚇 Red line: Chicago 🚌 157 🚻 Good 💰 Moderate; free first Tue of month

MUSEUM OF CONTEMPORARY PHOTOGRAPHY

In addition to the museum's own collection of American photography, you will find varied temporary exhibitions of contemporary photography from around the world.

➕ H7 ✉ 600 S Michigan Avenue ☎ 312/663 5554 🕐 Mon–Fri 10–5; Sat noon–5 🚇 Red line: Harrison 🚌 1, 3, 4, 6, 38, 146 🚻 Good 💰 Free

ERNEST HEMINGWAY MUSEUM

A collection remembering the Nobel-Prize-winning writer who spent his first 18 years in Oak Park. Open the same hours and on the the same street, at number 339 N, is Hemingway's birthplace.

➕ Off map to west ✉ 200 N Oak Park Avenue ☎ 708/848 2222
🕐 Fri and Sun 1–5; Sat 10–5. Closed Mon–Thu 🚇 Blue line: Harlem
🚌 23 🚉 Oak Park ♿ Few 💲 Moderate

DAVID AND ALFRED SMART MUSEUM OF ART

An eclectic collection, with works by Auguste Rodin, Albrecht Dürer and Mark Rothko, and furniture from Frank Lloyd Wright.

➕ Off map ✉ 5550 S Greenwood Avenue ☎ 312/702 0200
🕐 Tue–Fri noon–4; Sat–Sun noon–6 🚇 Red line: Garfield 🚌 4
🚉 59th Street ♿ Good 💲 Donations

SPERTUS MUSEUM OF JUDAICA

Torah scrolls, Hanukkah lamps and tools used in circumcision are among the decorative and religious objects spanning 5,000 years that form the core of this museum's extensive collection of Judaica. However, only a small selection can be shown at any one time. The richness of most exhibits contrasts strongly with the sombre collection of Holocaust memorabilia.

➕ H7 ✉ 618 S Michigan Avenue
☎ 312/922 9012
🕐 Sun–Thu 10–5; Fri 10–3 🚇 Red line: Harrison 🚌 1, 3, 4, 6, 38, 146 ♿ Good
💲 Moderate; free Fri

National Vietnam Veteran's Art Museum

Paintings, sculpture, writing and photography from (mostly) American combatants in the Vietnam War fill this museum (✉ 1801 S Indiana Avenue). Adding to the sense of despair evoked by many works are the guns and equipment, used by both sides, that share the gallery space. The effect can be harrowing; one reviewer called the collection 'art in a state of shock'.

An exhibit from the Spertus Museum

HISTORIC BUILDINGS

Marquette Building

Completed in 1895, the Marquette Building (⊠ 140 S Dearborn Street) is among the unsung masterpieces of Chicago architecture. It demonstrates the first use of the three-part 'Chicago Window' – plate glass spans the whole width between the building's steel supports. Lobby reliefs record the expedition of French Jesuit missionary Jacques Marquette; the entrance doors' panther heads are by Edward Kemeys, who is also responsible for the lions fronting the Art Institute of Chicago (► 40).

CLARKE HOUSE (1830s)

The Clarke House (named after its original owner), is the oldest structure in Chicago. The interior has been restored to a mid-19th-century appearance.
✚ H9 ⊠ 1800 S Prairie Avenue ☎ 312/326 1480 ⏰ Guided tours: Wed–Sun noon, 1, 2. Guided tours including Glessner House: Fri noon; Sat–Sun noon, 1, 2, 3 ⓠ Red line: Cermak/Chinatown 🚌 1, 3, 4, 18 🚉 18th Street ♿ Few ⓦ Moderate; can be combined with Glessner House

HISTORIC WATER TOWER (1869)

This pseudo-Gothic confection in yellow limestone, by William Boyington, is a celebrated city landmark.
✚ H5 ⊠ 800 N Michigan Avenue ☎ Ground-floor Tourist Information Center: 312/744 2400 ⏰ Mon–Sat 10–6; Sun noon–5 ⓠ Red line: Chicago 🚌 11, 66, 145, 146, 147, 151 ♿ Few ⓦ Free

RELIANCE BUILDING (1895)

Charles Atwood pre-empted the modern skyscraper with this building's steel skeleton and large bay windows divided by slim terracotta mullions.
✚ H6 ⊠ 32 N State Street ⓠ Red or Blue lines: Washington 🚌 20, 22, 36, 56

ROBIE HOUSE (1910)

A famed example of Frank Lloyd Wright's Prairie School style of architecture. The horizontal emphasis reflects the Midwest's open spaces.
✚ Off map ⊠ 5757 S Woodlawn Avenue ☎ 708/848 1976 ⏰ Guided tours: Mon–Fri 11, 1, 3. Continuous tours: Sat–Sun 11–3:30 ⓠ Green Line: Cottage Grove 🚌 4 🚉 59th Street ♿ Few ⓦ Free

The Historic Water Tower

MODERN BUILDINGS

**See Top 25 Sights for
SEARS TOWER (▶ 30)**

IBM BUILDING (1971)
The 54 storeys of Mies van der Rohe's last office building rise sleekly above the Chicago River. His bust is in the lobby.

➕ H6 ✉ 330 N Wabash Drive 🚇 Red line: Grand 🚌 29 ♿ Good

JAMES R THOMPSON CENTER (1985)
This glass and steel edifice was designed by Helmut Jahn. Inside, a soaring atrium is lined with shops, restaurants and cafés; upper levels house state agencies.

➕ G6 ✉ 100 W Randolph Street ☎ 312/814 2141 🚇 Blue, Brown, Orange lines: Clark/Lake 🚌 156 ♿ Good

James R Thompson Center's massive atrium

JOHN HANCOCK CENTER (1970)
The tapering profile of the John Hancock Center (designed by Skidmore, Owings & Merrill) is a feature of Chicago's skyline; until 1974, when Sears Tower was completed, it was the world's tallest building. It has an observatory (▶ 58).

➕ H4 ✉ 875 N Michigan Avenue ☎ 312/751 3681 🕐 Skydeck Observatory: daily 9AM–midnight 🚇 Red line: Chicago 🚌 145, 146, 147, 151 ♿ Good 💵 Skydeck Observatory: moderate

RICHARD J DALEY CENTER (1965)
Jacque Brownson (of C F Murphy Associates) is credited with the centre's design. Chiefly notable are the lobby's eternal flame memorial to the former mayor after whom the building is named, and the plaza's perplexing, untitled 1967 Picasso sculpture.

➕ G6 ✉ 50 W Washington Street 🚇 Blue line: Washington 🚌 6, 11, 20, 23, 56 ♿ Good

333 W WACKER DRIVE (1983)
The New York firm of Kohn Pedersen Fox struck a blow for post-modernism in Chicago with this acclaimed 36-storey building, which is slotted ingeniously into a triangular site next to the river.

➕ G6 ✉ 333 W Wacker Drive 🚇 Blue, Brown, Orange lines: Clark/Lake 🚌 16, 41, 125

Mies van der Rohe in Chicago

German-born Ludwig Mies van der Rohe, father of the International Style of architecture and one-time director of the German design school known as the Bauhaus, settled in Chicago in the 1940s, teaching at the Illinois Institute of Technology and redesigning it at the same time. Aside from the IBM Building and the institute, his most celebrated Chicago works are the glass and steel apartment buildings at 860–80 N Lake Shore Drive.

55

PLACES OF WORSHIP

Holy Name Cathedral

See Excursions for BAHA'I TEMPLE (▶ 20)

FOURTH PRESBYTERIAN CHURCH (1914)
This Gothic Revival church serves a congregation drawn from Chicago's moneyed élite. Occasional but enjoyable lunchtime concerts pack the pews.

✛ H4 ✉ 126 E Chestnut Street ☎ 312/787 4570 🚊 Red line: Chicago 🚌 145, 146, 147, 151 ♿ Good

HOLY NAME CATHEDRAL (1878)
The atmospheric seat of the Catholic Archdiocese of Chicago. In 1926, gangster and former choirboy 'Hymie' Weiss was machine-gunned to death on the steps.

✛ H5 ✉ 735 N State Street ☎ 312/787 8040 🚊 Red line: Chicago 🚌 29, 36 ♿ Good

ST NICHOLAS CATHEDRAL (1915)
A Byzantine-style cathedral, modelled on the Basilica of St Sophia in Kiev, and serving Chicago Ukrainians. The cathedral adopted the Gregorian calendar only in 1969, and then amid great opposition.

✛ C5 ✉ Junction of N Oakley Boulevard and W Rice Street ☎ 312/276 4537 🚊 Blue line: Chicago 🚌 66 ♿ Few

Quigley Seminary and St James Chapel

An array of Gothic buildings, complete with leering gargoyles, lines a courtyard on Rush Street – west of the Magnificent Mile, between E Chestnut and E Pearson streets. Completed in the mid-1920s, the complex forms the Quigley Seminary and includes the St James Chapel, decorated with stained-glass windows.

ST STANISLAUS KOSTKA CHURCH (1881)
Raised to serve Chicago's Polish immigrants, this Renaissance-style church quickly established the world's largest Catholic congregation.

✛ B4 ✉ 1351 W Evergreen Avenue ☎ Polish Museum of America: 312/278 2470 🚊 Blue line: Damen 🚌 52 ♿ Few

UNITY TEMPLE (1905)
Working to a tight budget, Frank Lloyd Wright used undecorated, reinforced concrete blocks – assembled into a series of interlocking sections – to create this temple for a Unitarian congregation. The furniture that Wright also designed for the building is still in use.

✛ Off map ✉ 875 Lake Street, Oak Park ☎ 708/383 8873 🕐 Memorial Day–Labor Day Mon–Fri 10–5. Rest of year Mon–Fri 1–4. Guided tours daily 🚊 Blue line: Harlem 🚌 23 🚃 Oak Park ♿ Few

PARKS, GARDENS & BEACHES

See Top 25 Sights for
GRANT PARK (► 41)
LINCOLN PARK (► 29)

JACKSON PARK
In 1893, 27 million people attended the World's
Columbian Exposition, held in what became Jackson
Park, now a pleasant green space with sports courts, a
Japanese garden, and the Museum of Science and
Industry (► 48).
🚻 Off map to south ✉ Between S Stony Island Avenue and Lake
Michigan 🚇 Red line: Garfield 🚌 6, 10 🚆 55th, 56th, 57th Street

NORTH AVENUE BEACH
The mile-long North Avenue Beach draws a cross-
section of the city's population, and is ideal for lazy
sunbathing. Volleyball nets are provided and there
is a 1950s chess pavilion at the southern end of the
beach.
🚻 G/H1–3 ✉ Accessed from Lincoln Park 🚌 145, 146, 147,
151, 156

OAK PARK CONSERVATORY
Waterfalls, a herb garden, and assorted desert and
tropical vegetation are among the highlights of this
under-visited park.
🚻 Off map ✉ 615 Garfield Street, Oak Park 🚇 Blue line: Oak Park
Avenue 🚌 23 🚆 Oak Park

OAK STREET BEACH
The closeness of the
exclusive Gold Coast
neighbourhood helps
make Oak Street Beach
the gathering place for
some of Chicago's richest
and best-toned bodies.
🚻 H4 ✉ Pedestrian access from
junction of N Michigan Avenue and
E Lake Shore Drive 🚌 145, 146,
147, 151

WASHINGTON SQUARE
This was Chicago's first
public park, and once
buzzed with Sunday
afternoon soap-box
orators. Lunching office
workers and shoppers are
now its main users.
🚻 G4 ✉ Bordered by W Walton
Street and Delaware Place, and
N Clark and N Dearborn streets
🚇 Red line: Chicago 🚌 22

Garfield Park
Conservatory
Providing a refuge from urban
Chicago, the conservatory
(✉ 300 N Central Park
Boulevard) has 5 acres of tropical
and subtropical plants, and is open
daily, 9–5, all year round. The
highlights include extensive
collections of palms, ferns and
cacti. Chicagoans come here for
expert gardening tips and for
shows, when the opening hours
are extended.

*A sweeping view of the
Chicago beaches*

VIEWS

See Top 25 Sights for
SKYDECK, SEARS TOWER (▶ 30)

BOAT TOURS
Almost any boat tour (▶ 19) brings fabulous views of the Loop's architecture, and the rest of the city strung along the Lake Michigan shoreline.

THE EL
As they loop the Loop from elevated rails, El trains on the Brown line bring spectacular close-up views of the district's high-rise architecture, its streets and its car parks, from unexpected angles.
✚ G/H6/7

The view from John Hancock Center's Skydeck Observatory

JOHN HANCOCK CENTER SKYDECK OBSERVATORY
Many Chicagoans prefer this 94th-floor outlook (over 1,000ft high, and close to other buildings and the lake) to the slightly higher, but much busier, Sears Tower Skydeck (▶ 30).
✚ H4 ✉ 875 N Michigan Avenue
☎ 888/875 VIEW 🕓 Skydeck Observatory: daily 9AM–midnight
🚇 Red line: Chicago 🚌 145, 146, 147, 151 ♿ Good 💵 Moderate

MICHIGAN AVENUE BRIDGE
Night-time on this Chicago River crossing point reveals the Wrigley Building and Tribune Tower illuminated by floodlights; in the other direction loom the variously lit high-rises of the Loop.
✚ H5/6 ✉ Michigan Avenue between E Wacker Drive and E Illinois Street

Sunrise and the Lakefront Trail

Earlybirds can enjoy one of the best sunrises anywhere in the Midwest by joining the walkers, joggers and cyclists who start each morning on the 10-mile Lakefront Trail through Lincoln Park (▶ 29). The spectacle created as the sun comes up over the lake, its rays reflected in the buildings of the Loop, makes the effort to be there well worth while.

LAKE SHORE DRIVE
By car, the best views of Chicago's high-rise skyline are from Lake Shore Drive, which cuts between the city and Lake Michigan. Passengers will relish the spectacle, though on weekdays drivers might well be too preoccupied with negotiating some of the worst of Chicago's traffic to enjoy the splendid outlook.

PROMONTORY POINT
From this lakeside outlook some 5 miles south of the Loop, the Chicago skyline rises in great splendour. To the east, the curving Lake Michigan shoreline marks the northern edge of Indiana.
✚ Off map to south ✉ Eastern end of 55th Street

ATTRACTIONS FOR CHILDREN

ARTiFACT CENTER AT THE SPERTUS MUSEUM

Interactive exhibits guide inquisitive minds through the mysteries of Middle Eastern archaeology, and a re-created dig allows young hands to 'discover' buried items from early Jewish civilisations, described in wall charts, maps and explanatory texts.

➕ H7 ✉ 618 S Michigan Avenue ☎ 312/922 9012 ⏰ Sun–Thu 10–5; Fri 10–3 🚇 Red line: Harrison 🚌 1, 3, 4, 6, 38, 146 ♿ Good 💲 Moderate

CHICAGO ACADEMY OF SCIENCES – THE NATURE MUSEUM

Lively exhibits explore the natural history of the Midwest, including walk-through caverns and the inside story on the formation of the Great Lakes. Due to move in 1999 to Lincoln Park.

➕ J5 ✉ North Pier, 435 E Illinois Street until completion of new purpose-built museum (expected in 1999) ☎ 773/871 2668 ⏰ Mon–Fri 9:30–4:30; Sat 10–6; Sun noon–6 🚇 Red line: Grand 🚌 29, 56, 65, 66 ♿ Good 💲 Moderate; free Tue

CHICAGO CHILDREN'S MUSEUM

Spread across three floors are scores of lively and entertaining things to do for those aged under 12. These include workshop areas such as the Inventing Lab, where kids can assemble flying machines, and Artabounds, where they can create murals and sculptures. Programmes change daily.

➕ J5 ✉ Navy Pier, 700 E Grand Avenue ☎ 312/527 1000 ⏰ Tue–Sun 10–5; Thu 10–4, 5–8 🚇 Red line: Grand 🚌 29, 56, 65, 66 ♿ Good 💲 Moderate; free Thu 5–8

LINCOLN PARK ZOO

Lions, cheetahs, gorillas and chimpanzees are especially popular, along with the Children's Zoo, where tame and usually very furry animals can be stroked and cuddled.

➕ G2 ✉ Lincoln Park ☎ 312/742 2000 ⏰ Daily 9–5 🚇 Brown line: Armitage, Fullerton. Red line: Fullerton 🚌 151, 156 ♿ Few 💲 Free

The Farm-in-the-Zoo

You'll find chickens, cows and sheep at the Farm-in-the-Zoo section of Lincoln Park Zoo, a 5-acre re-creation of a Midwest farm. Milking and butter-making are among the activities demonstrated, and they seldom fail to intrigue city-dwellers of all ages.

Fun and games at the Chicago Children's Museum

FREE ATTRACTIONS

Watching the money-go-round

Speculating on pork belly futures is just one speciality of Chicago's financial dealers. At the Chicago Board of Trade (➤ 31) and the Mercantile Exchange (✉ 30 S Wacker Drive) visitors who love the sight of money changing hands, but do not want to risk a cent, can watch from public galleries as millions of dollars are made and lost.

HAROLD WASHINGTON LIBRARY CENTER

The US's largest public library is a state-of-the-art facility. Note its free exhibitions and eye-catching artworks. It has a children's library too.

➕ H7 ✉ 400 S State Street ☎ 312/747 4876 🕐 Mon 9–7; Tue and Thu 11–7; Wed, Fri–Sat 9–5; Sun 1–5 🚇 Blue line: La Salle 🚌 11, 145, 146, 147 ♿ Good

LOOP SCULPTURES

Impressive sculptures on many plazas of the Loop include those by Alexander Calder (✉ Federal Center, Dearborn Street), Joan Miró (✉ Washington Street), Marc Chagall (✉ First National Plaza, Dearborn Street) and Jean Dubuffet (✉ James R Thompson Center; ➤ 16, 55).

➕ G/H6/7

Alexander Calder's Flamingo at the Loop

MEXICAN FINE ARTS CENTER MUSEUM

Displaying selections from a permanent collection of some 1,200 works by artists of Mexican nationality or descent, this museum also mounts strong and varied temporary exhibitions.

➕ D9 ✉ 1852 W 19th Street ☎ 312/738 1503 🕐 Tue–Sun 10–5 🚇 Blue line: 18th Street 🚌 18 ♿ Good

NAVY PIER

The 1916 Navy Pier has been rejuvenated with cafés, restaurants, nightclubs, museums and speciality shops.

➕ J/K5 ✉ 600 E Grand Avenue ☎ 312/595 PIER 🕐 Businesses have individual hours 🚇 Red line: Grand 🚌 29, 56, 65, 66 ♿ Good

NORTH PIER

Like Navy Pier, this now offers a feast of shops, eateries and other forms of amusement.

➕ J5 ✉ 435 E Illinois Street ☎ 312/836 4300 🕐 Businesses have individual hours 🚇 Red line: Grand 🚌 29, 56, 65, 66 ♿ Good

CHICAGO's
where to...

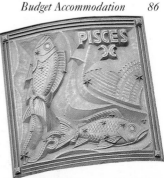

61

CONTEMPORARY AMERICAN

Prices

Average meal per person
excluding drinks

£ = Up to $15

££ = $15–30

£££ = $30–$50

£££ = Above $50

All the restaurants listed are
open daily for lunch and dinner
unless otherwise stated.

At the luxury restaurants on this
page, the cost of dinner will
easily exceed $70 excluding
wine for two people, and lunch
will typically cost around $50.
Except in these luxury
restaurants, dining in Chicago is
often less expensive than in
other major American cities.
Expect to spend $6–$9 per
person for breakfast, $8–$14
for lunch and $15–$25 for
dinner excluding drinks and tip.
A tip of at least 15 per cent is
expected; reward good service
with 20 per cent or more.

Topolobambo
(££–£££)

Chef Rick Bayless reaches new
heights with his bold,
imaginative haute Mexican
cuisine at Topolobambo.

⊞ G5 ⊠ 445 N Clark Street
☎ 312/661 1434 🕐 No
lunch Fri. Closed Sun–Mon
🚇 Blue line: Clark, Lake
🚌 22

AMBRIA (££££)

A seasonally varied
menu mating cuisines
of France and the
world. The impeccable
service matches the
immaculate setting,
formerly part of a very
upper-crust hotel.

⊞ G2 ⊠ 2300 N Lincoln Park
West ☎ 312/472 5959
🕐 Dinner only. Closed Sun
🚇 Brown line: Sedgwick
🚌 156

CAFÉ ABSINTHE (££)

Dark, atmospheric and
swanky, and excellent
eclectic American
cuisine with surprisingly
little attitude. Go early
to avoid the crowds or
late to people-watch.

⊞ C3 ⊠ 1954 W North
Avenue ☎ 773/278 4488
🕐 Dinner only 🚇 Blue line:
Damen 🚌 50, 56, 73

CHARLIE TROTTER'S
(£££)

A fashionable dining
place with superbly
inventive, and
sometimes eccentric
cooking, with care
lavished on everything,
down to the smallest
detail.

⊞ F2 ⊠ 816 W Armitage
Avenue ☎ 312/248 6228
🕐 Dinner only. Closed Sun, Mon
🚇 Brown line: Armitage
🚌 8, 73

GORDON (£££)

Owner Gordon Sinclair
has been treating
patrons to his own brand
of sophisticated dining
since 1976. A Chicago
classic.

⊞ G5 ⊠ 500 N Clark Street
☎ 312/467 9780 🕐 No lunch
Sat–Wed 🚇 Red line: Grand
Avenue 🚌 22

PRINTER'S ROW (£££)

American regional fare
rises to new heights
here. Game and seafood
are specialities.

⊞ G7 ⊠ 550 S Dearborn
Street ☎ 312/461 0780
🕐 No lunch on Sat. Closed Sun
🚇 Red line: Harrison 🚌 24,
36

SEASONS (£££)

Food that is at once
complex and comforting,
served in a luxurious
setting. Wonderful
wines by the glass.

⊞ H4 ⊠ Four Seasons Hotel,
120 E Delaware Place
☎ 312/649 2349
🕐 Breakfast, dinner. No lunch
Sun 🚇 Red line: Chicago
🚌 145, 146, 147, 151

SPAGO (££££)

This spin-off of the
famous Los Angeles
restaurant has become
a premier dining
destination. The food,
from chef François
Kwaku-Dongo, is
exotically accented
international.

⊞ G5 ⊠ 520 N Dearborn
Street ☎ 312/527 3700
🕐 No lunch Sun 🚇 Red line:
Grand Avenue 🚌 22, 36, 65

TRIO (££££)

Chef Shawn McLain
provides a truly
memorable experience
with startling
presentations and
flavours to match. One
of the most coveted
reservations in town.

⊞ Off map ⊠ 1625 Hinman
Avenue, Evanston ☎ 847/733
8746 🕐 No lunch Sat–Thu
🚇 Purple line: Davis Street

STEAKS, RIBS & CHOPS

CHICAGO CHOP HOUSE (££–£££)

The ribs, steaks and chops here are large and juicy enough to satisfy even the most demanding red-meat eaters. All meals begin with a fresh green salad and a loaf of wholemeal bread.

➕ G5 ✉ 60 W Ontario Street ☎ 312/787 7100 🕐 No lunch on Sat and Sun Ⓜ Red line: Grand 🚌 125

ELI'S THE PLACE FOR STEAK (££–£££)

This is a noted spot for perfectly cooked T-bone steaks. Try not to miss the cheesecake; the liver-and-onion appetizer is worth tasting, too.

➕ H5 ✉ 215 E Chicago Avenue ☎ 312/642 1393 🕐 No lunch Sat–Sun Ⓜ Red line: Chicago 🚌 3, 66

GENE & GEORGETTI (£££)

Many feel that this steakhouse – complete with the men's-club décor, gruff waiters and deliciously thick cuts of meat – is the best in the city. Non-carnivores beware – the menu offers scant choices for you.

➕ G5 ✉ 500 N Franklin Street ☎ 312/527 3718 Ⓜ Brown, Purple lines: Merchandise Mart 🚌 20

LAWRY'S THE PRIME RIB (££–£££)

The primest of prime rib – the only option on the dinner menu here – is accompanied by such traditional favourites as Yorkshire pudding, mashed potato and salad or an enormous baked potato.

➕ H5 ✉ 100 E Ontario Street ☎ 312/787 5000 🕐 No lunch at weekends Ⓜ Red line: Grand 🚌 125

MORTON'S (££–£££)

Steak is taken seriously in Chicago, and this is one of the best places to eat it. Porterhouse steaks grilled to perfection are the stock-in-trade.

➕ H4 ✉ 1050 N State Street ☎ 312/266 4820 🕐 Dinner only Ⓜ Red line: Chicago 🚌 36

ROBINSON'S NO 1 RIBS (£–££)

A favourite for barbecued ribs, chicken, beef and pork, served with a choice of sauces, plus coleslaw and beans.

➕ F2 ✉ 655 W Armitage Avenue ☎ 312/337 1399 🕐 No lunch at weekends Ⓜ Brown line: Armitage 🚌 73

RUTH'S CHRIS STEAKHOUSE (££–£££)

The Chicago branch of the biggest steakhouse chain in the US opened in 1992 and quickly made its mark. It serves substantial steaks, lamb, veal and pork, all topped with sizzling butter.

➕ G6 ✉ 431 N Dearborn Street ☎ 312/321 2725 🕐 No lunch on Sat. Closed Sun Ⓜ Blue, Red lines: Jackson 🚌 22, 36

Brunch

A mix of late breakfast and early lunch, brunch is a popular Sunday event in the US. Brunch is usually served from 10AM to 2PM and typically costs $10–$20, depending on the surroundings and the combination of food and drink included. The restaurant sections of local newspapers and magazines have plenty of brunch suggestions; reservations are strongly advised.

Quick Bites & Tapas

Chicago hot dogs

To a Chicagoan, a hot dog is
not merely a sausage in a bun.
The true Chicago hot dog is a
Viennese beef sausage smeared
with ketchup, mustard, relish,
onions and hot peppers to taste.
Brightly lit hot-dog outlets are a
feature of the city and each has
its devotees. If you have
gourmet pretensions, sample a
branch of Gold Coast Dogs –
heaven for enthusiasts of hot
dogs with all the trimmings.

✚ H5 ✉ 418 N State Street,
and other locations throughout
the city ☎ 312/527 1222
🕐 Breakfast, lunch, dinner.
Closed Sat–Sun 🚇 Red line:
Grand 🚌 29, 36

ANN SATHER'S (£)
A venerable coffee shop
where Swedish fare,
such as cranberry
pancakes, tops the list of
usual diner favourites.
✚ Off map ✉ 929 W Belmont
Avenue ☎ 773/348 2378
🕐 Breakfast, lunch, dinner
🚇 Brown, Red lines: Belmont
🚌 77

BIG BOWL CAFÉ (£–££)
Delectable Asian noodle
dishes, and much more,
served in very big bowls.
Owner Oprah Winfrey is
elusive.
✚ G5 ✉ 159 1/2 W Erie
Street ☎ 312/787 8297
🕐 No lunch Sun 🚇 Brown
line: Chicago 🚌 37, 41

CAFÉ IBERICO (£–££)
Tapas, plus a full menu
with Spanish regional
specialities. Good
selection of Spanish
wines.
✚ G5 ✉ 737 N La Salle Street
☎ 312/573 1510 🚇 Brown
line: Chicago 🚌 11, 156

ED DEBEVIC'S SHORT
ORDER DELUXE (£–££)
Great burgers,
sandwiches, and
milkshakes, plus music
of the 1950s and 1960s.
✚ G5 ✉ 640 N Wells Street
☎ 312/664 1707
🕐 Breakfast, lunch, dinner
🚇 Brown line: Chicago
🚌 37, 41

LAKEFRONT
RESTAURANT (£)
Wonderful soups and
sandwiches, plus other
hearty fare served in a
lively atmosphere.
✚ Off map ✉ 3042 N
Broadway ☎ 773/472 9040
🕐 Breakfast, lunch, dinner
🚇 Brown line: Diversey 🚌 36

LOU MITCHELL'S (£)
A modestly sized and
friendly diner, founded
in the 1930s and still
serving great omelettes
and other dishes.
✚ F7 ✉ 565 W Jackson
Boulevard ☎ 312/939 3111
🕐 Breakfast and lunch only.
Closed Sun 🚇 Blue line: Clinton
🚌 7, 126

THE MELROSE (£)
A coffee shop whose
clientele ranges from
breakfasting manual
workers to snacking
nightclubbers.
Enormous menu.
✚ Off map ✉ 3233 N
Broadway ☎ 773/327 2060
🕐 Breakfast, lunch, dinner
🚇 Brown, Red lines: Belmont
🚌 36

SOUL KITCHEN (£)
A favourite of soul food
aficionados. New
Orleans-inspired food
and casually charged
atmosphere.
✚ C3 ✉ 1547 N Milwaukee
Avenue ☎ 773/342 9742
🕐 No lunch 🚇 Blue line:
Damen 🚌 27, 56, 60

TWIN ANCHORS (£–££)
Simply the best place
for ribs, and once a
hangout of Al Capone's.
Go early.
✚ G3 ✉ 1655 Sedgwick
Street ☎ 312/266 1616
🕐 No lunch Mon–Fri 🚇 Red
line: Clybourn. Brown line:
Sedgwick 🚌 37

WISHBONE (£)
Authentic soul food and
Cajun specialities at this
interesting down-home
joint.
✚ F6 ✉ 1001 W Washington
Street ☎ 312/850 2663
🕐 Closed Sun–Mon 🚌 20

GERMAN & EAST EUROPEAN

BERGHOFF RESTAURANT (£–££)

German staples such as *sauerbraten* and *bratwurst* are served in a cavernous oak-panelled dining room, along with home-brewed German-style beer. Well-prepared American dishes are also available on the menu. The Berghoff is one of Chicago's long-standing institutions, founded in 1893.

✚ H7 ✉ 17 W Adams Street ☎ 312/427 3170 ⏰ Closed Sun 🚇 Blue, Red lines: Jackson 🚌 1, 7, 60, 126, 151

BUSY BEE (£)

A slice of real neighbourhood life – as well as cheap Polish food – can be enjoyed at this very convivial locals' spot, which is located right in the heart of Chicago's substantial Polish and Ukrainian communities.

✚ C3 ✉ 1546 N Damen Avenue ☎ 773/772 4433 ⏰ Breakfast, lunch, dinner 🚇 Blue line: Damen 🚌 50

MAREVA'S (£££)

Excellent Polish fare served in an elegant setting. Be sure to try the Polish stuffed pastries known as *pierogi*: these are some of the best examples available in the city.

✚ D4 ✉ 1250 N Milwaukee Avenue ☎ 773/227 4000 ⏰ No lunch weekdays. Closed Mon 🚇 Blue line: Division 🚌 56

RUSSIAN TEA CAFÉ (££)

Caviar, roast pheasant, iced Vodka and other gastric specialities from Russia and its neighbours in the former Soviet Union.

✚ H7 ✉ 77 E Adams Street ☎ 312/360 0000 ⏰ Lunch only on Mon 🚇 Brown, Orange lines: Adams 🚌 1, 7, 60, 126, 151

SAK'S UKRAINIAN VILLAGE RESTAURANT (£)

A lively restaurant and a favourite for traditional Ukrainian fare, including stuffed cabbage, chicken Kiev, substantial soups and wonderful sweet *blintzes*.

✚ C5 ✉ 2301 W Chicago Avenue ☎ 773/278 4445 ⏰ Closed Mon 🚇 Blue line: Damen 🚌 66

ZUM DEUTSCHEN ECK (££)

This German restaurant feels like a Bavarian beer hall, and draws a strong German-American contingent. At weekends, Chicago's best oompah band is to hand. Waitresses in traditional costume.

✚ Off map ✉ 2924 N Southport Avenue ☎ 773/525 8121 🚇 Brown line: Paulina 🚌 9

The Taste of Chicago

Chicagoans love to eat and do so with gusto by the thousand at the Taste of Chicago festival, held in Grant Park annually. For eight days before 4 July around 100 local restaurants dispense their creations at affordable prices from impromptu stalls. Free musical entertainment helps make the festival one of the city's most eagerly awaited annual events.

FRENCH & ITALIAN

FRENCH

THE DINING ROOM (££££)
Spread across two sumptuously furnished floors of this luxury hotel and offering matchless contemporary French cuisine from the *carte* or as a fixed-price meal.
🚹 H5 ✉ Ritz-Carlton Hotel, 160 E Pearson Street
☎ 312/266 1000 🕐 Dinner only 🚇 Red line: Chicago
🚌 125, 157

EVEREST (££££)
This 40th-floor restaurant, beloved of financial wheeler-dealers, offers an updated and sometimes inspiring look at chef Jean Joho's native Alsace. The location, prices and standards of cooking are all breathtakingly high.
🚹 G7 ✉ 440 S La Salle Street
☎ 312/663 8920 🕐 Dinner only. Closed Sun, Mon 🚇 Blue line: La Salle 🚌 22

LE FRANÇAIS (££££)
Since the 1970s, the impeccable fare and extraordinary wine list have been drawing diners to this culinary destination about an hour outside the city.
🚹 Off map ✉ 269 Milwaukee Avenue, Wheeling ☎ 847/541 7470 🕐 No lunch Sat–Mon. Closed Sun ❓ Best reached by car

ITALIAN

BACINO'S STUFFED PIZZA (£–££)
Loop branch of city-wide chain; the house speciality is a tasty spinach pizza served with a choice of cheeses.
🚹 H6 ✉ 75 E Wacker Drive
☎ 312/263 0070 🚇 Brown, Orange lines: State 🚌 16, 44

BERTUCCI'S BRICK OVEN PIZZERIA (£–££)
Upbeat décor, a vivacious crowd, and deeply flavourful pizzas cooked in huge brick ovens.
🚹 G5 ✉ 675 N La Salle Street
☎ 312/266 3400 🚇 Brown line: Chicago 🚌 11, 156

COCO PAZZO (££–£££)
Delectable, mostly northern Italian regional cuisine presented in a comfortable setting; the menu includes tremendous daily specials and mouth-watering desserts. Customers enjoy a good view of their dishes being prepared in the kitchen.
🚹 G5 ✉ 300 W Hubbard Street
☎ 312/836 0900 🕐 No lunch at weekends 🚇 Red line: Grand
🚌 11, 156

EDWARDO'S NATURAL PIZZA (£–££)
One of several Chicago branches of a fast-growing chain devoted to serving healthy, nutritious pizzas seasoned with home-grown basil.
🚹 G4 ✉ 1212 N Dearborn Street ☎ 312/337 4490
🚇 Red line: Clark/Division
🚌 11, 70

Dining with children
Most Chicago restaurants welcome children, and many provide small colouring sets and toys to keep them amused. There are often children's menus offering scaled-down portions and the sort of fare that many children prefer such as burgers, French fries and ice cream.

GINO'S EAST (£)

Some of Chicago's finest deep-dish pizza is served here in a no-frills setting. Expect to find crowds here during meal hours.

H5 ⊠ 160 E Superior Street ☎ 312/943 1124 ⊕ Red line: Chicago 🚌 3, 11, 125, 145, 146, 147, 151

GRAPPA (££–£££)

A formidable range of Italian fare served up in a post-modern setting. The linguini with calamari and grilled shrimp are enticing. Excellent service.

H4 ⊠ 200 E Chestnut Street ☎ 312/337 4500 ⊕ Red line: Chicago 🚌 36, 125

LA STRADA (££)

Well-presented, mostly northern Italian fare, served beneath crystal chandeliers in a very elegant setting.

H6 ⊠ 155 N Michigan Avenue ☎ 312/565 2200 ⊕ Brown, Orange lines: Randolph 🚌 38, 56, 156

LOU MALNATI'S PIZZERIA (£)

Casual, fun place serving an excellent version of traditional deep-dish pizza. Quintessential Chicago.

G5 ⊠ 439 N Wells Street ☎ 312/828 9800 ⊕ Brown line: Merchandise Mart 🚌 37, 65, 156

MIA FRANCESCA (££)

There is always a wait at this favourite of Chicago natives. Excellent seafood specials and wonderful red-sauced fare.

🚌 Off map ⊠ 3311 N Clark Street ☎ 773/281 3310 ⊕ Dinner only ⊕ Brown, Red, Purple lines: Belmont 🚌 22

SCOOZI! (££)

A vivacious spot for inventive Italian fare, Scoozi! is huge and often crowded – it is very popular with a young crowd. It is easy to recognise – look out for the giant tomato hanging over the door.

G5 ⊠ 410 W Huron Street ☎ 312/943 5900 ⊕ No lunch Sun ⊕ Brown line: Chicago 🚌 37, 41

SPIAGGIA (£££)

Steamed mussels in garlic-and-tomato broth is just one of the specialities provided in this celebrity favourite. The adjoining Spiaggia Café is a less costly, less formal branch, and serves a range of excellent pizza and pasta dishes.

H4 ⊠ 980 N Michigan Avenue ☎ 312/280 2750 ⊕ Dinner only on Sun ⊕ Red line: Chicago 🚌 145, 146, 147, 151

VINCI (££)

Fashionable décor and rustic cuisine make Vinci top of the list for many natives. It can be noisy, but the staff are attentive.

F3 ⊠ 1732 N Halstead Street ☎ 312/266 1199 ⊕ Dinner Tue–Sun; brunch Sun. Closed Mon ⊕ Red line: North Avenue, Clybourn 🚌 20, 72

Chicago pizza

The first deep-dish pizza was created in 1943 at Chicago's Pizzeria Uno (H5 ⊠ 29 E Ohio Street ☎ 312/321 1000 ⊕ Red line: Grand 🚌 36). The thick but light crust and a generous smothering of tomato sauce and mozzarella cheese, combined with a variety of toppings, helped make the Chicago pizza a full meal in itself, unlike the thin-crusted New York version. Pizzeria Uno (£) is deservedly as popular as ever. There is now a second branch, Pizzeria Due, at H6 ⊠ 610 N Wabash Avenue.

67

ASIAN & INDIAN

Dim sum

Served by many Chinese restaurants at lunchtime, *dim sum* is the term for a range of small dishes wheeled round on trolleys. Stop a server who has dishes that look appetising – and take your pick. Popular dishes include *cha sil bow* – steamed pork bun; *gai bow* – steamed chicken bun; *chern goon* – spring rolls; and *sil mi* – steamed pork and shrimp dumpling. When sated, you will be charged by the plate.

ASIAN

EMPEROR'S CHOICE (££–£££)
Portraits of former Chinese emperors hang above diners who tuck into some of Chinatown's most creative seafood dishes. For a special occasion you can order Peking duck – but make sure you do so a day in advance.

✚ G10 ✉ 2238 S Wentworth Avenue ☎ 312/225 8800 🚇 Red line: Cermak/Chinatown 🚌 24

ITTO SUSHI (££)
Excellent and affordable *sushi* and *sashimi*, prepared before your eyes, are Itto Sushi's house speciality, but there is also a general menu of varied Japanese fare.

✚ F1 ✉ 2616 N Halsted Street ☎ 773/871 1800 🕐 Closed Sun 🚇 Brown line: Diversey 🚌 8

MANDAR INN (££)
An impressive array of fiery Szechwan dishes stands out amid the fare from the regions of China on a wide-ranging menu. Convivial atmosphere.

✚ G10 ✉ 2249 S Wentworth Avenue ☎ 312/842 4014 🕐 Closed Mon 🚇 Red line: Cermak/Chinatown 🚌 24

SZECHWAN EAST (££–£££)
Smart and stylish, and specialising in hot and zesty Szechwan dishes. The weekday lunch buffet is good value.

✚ H5 ✉ 340 E Ohio Street ☎ 312/255 9200 🚇 Red line: Grand 🚌 3, 66, 157

THREE HAPPINESS (£–££)
This is the right spot for a *dim sum* lunch or for brunch on Sunday, when it tends to fill up very quickly.

✚ G10 ✉ 2130 S Wentworth Avenue ☎ 312/791 1228 🚇 Red line: Cermak/Chinatown 🚌 24

INDIAN & SOUTHEAST ASIAN

ARUN'S (£££)
Superb Thai fare, with subtle spicing reflecting the exceptional flair of the kitchen.

✚ Off map ✉ 4156 N Kedzie Avenue ☎ 312/539 1909 🕐 Dinner only. Closed Mon 🚇 Brown line: Kedzie 🚌 80, 82

BUKHARA (£–££)
From the glass-walled kitchen come succulent tandoori dishes and other northwest India specialities; Indian bread is used instead of the usual eating utensils. It's worth trying the inexpensive buffet available for weekday lunch.

✚ H5 ✉ 2 E Ontario Street ☎ 312/943 0188 🚇 Red line: Grand 🚌 22

HUA GIANG (£–££)
Among the more elegant restaurants in this strongly Vietnamese neighbourhood, Hua Giang offers excellent value for money, from the crispy spring rolls to the more elaborate dishes.

➕ Off map ✉ 1104 W Argyle Street ☎ 773/275 8691 🕐 Closed Thu 🚇 Red line: Argyle 🚌 36

KLAY OVEN (£££)

Here, at one of Chicago's most acclaimed Indian restaurants, traditional dishes are expertly prepared and stylishly presented by attentive and friendly staff in a sumptuous setting. The menu also features some creative adaptations of popular American dishes.

➕ G5 ✉ 414 N Orleans Street ☎ 312/527 3999 🕐 No lunch at weekends. Closed Mon 🚇 Brown line: Merchandise Mart 🚌 37, 41

NHU HOA CAFÉ (£)

This is a small but welcoming spot, where you can sample an interesting range of Vietnamese and Laotian dishes.

➕ Off map ✉ 1020 W Argyle Street ☎ 773/878 0618 🕐 Closed Mon 🚇 Red line: Argyle 🚌 146

PATTAYA (£–££)

Exceptionally good, well-priced Thai eatery with an impressive selection of noodle dishes, plus curries and several other options. Let your server know how spicy you like your food.

➕ G5 ✉ 114 W Chicago Avenue ☎ 312/944 3753 🕐 Closed Sun 🚇 Red line: Chicago 🚌 22

PENNY'S NOODLE SHOP (£)

This Thai-inspired noodle shop draws raves from its many proponents. The menu features traditional dishes as well as creative interpretations. Delicious.

➕ Off map ✉ 3400 Sheffield Avenue ☎ 773/281 8222 🕐 Brown, Red, Purple lines: Belmont 🚌 7

STANDARD INDIA (£)

The utilitarian décor is not very promising, but the Indian food is good. Although you can choose dishes from the menu, many customers prefer to opt for the very cheap lunch and dinner buffet which is served daily.

➕ Off map ✉ 917 W Belmont Avenue ☎ 312/929 1123 🕐 Brown, Red lines: Belmont 🚌 77

THAI CLASSIC (£–££)

The low-cost lunch specials and wonderful Sunday buffet are well worth sampling, and the regular menu is no less impressive. Thai Classic doesn't have a licence to serve alcohol, but you are welcome to take your own bottle.

➕ Off map ✉ 3332 N Clark Street ☎ 312/404 2000 🕐 Red line: Addison 🚌 22

Vegetarian dining

Most Chinese, Thai and Vietnamese restaurants offer meat-free versions of their staples, as do Indian eateries; Italian restaurants (► 66–7) are another likely possibility. Even amid the chop houses and barbecued rib joints, vegetarians won't go hungry. Among the few exclusively vegetarian restaurants, try Café Voltaire (✉ 3231 N Clark Street).

MALLS & DEPARTMENT STORES

Chinatown shopping

For shoppers who venture from the better-known retail areas into Chinatown (▶ 50), rewards are plentiful in the form of entertaining emporia squeezed between the countless restaurants that line Wentworth Avenue immediately south of Cermak Road. They include Oriental Food Market (✉ 2002 S), stocked with edible delights, and Woks 'n' Things (✉ 2234 S), selling kitchen utensils and general gifts. Within a few strides, you can also pick up a bag of fortune cookies at Fortella (✉ 2252 S) and have your face or palm read at Nature Field (✉ 2351A S).

THE ATRIUM MALL
Diverse shops provide an excellent excuse to stroll around the spectacular second floor of this dazzling atrium, with its glass, marble and steel, and its impressive waterfall.
🔹 H6 ✉ James R Thompson Center, 100 W Randolph Street ☎ 312/346 0777 🚇 Blue, Brown, Orange lines: Clark/Lake 🚌 156

CARSON PIRIE SCOTT & CO STORE
Though better known for its exterior architecture (▶ 34), the store has provided middle-class Chicagoans with good clothing, cosmetics and household accessories for years.
🔹 H6 ✉ 1 S State Street ☎ 312/641 7000 🚇 Blue line: Madison. Red line: Monroe 🚌 22, 23, 36, 56, 157

CENTURY SHOPPING CENTER
This former theatre now houses a mixture of well-known chain stores, mostly clothing specialists, and intriguing locally based speciality shops. Many Chicagoans also come here to use the gym on the top floor.
🔹 F1 ✉ 2828 N Clark Street ☎ 773/929 8100 🚇 Brown line: Diversey 🚌 22, 36, 76

CHICAGO PLACE
A seven-floor branch of the excellent Saks Fifth Avenue department store is an anchor tenant among the classy retailers in this towering construction. Drop into Chiasso to admire artworks and ornaments, explore the Slavic gifts and art in Russian Creations, or snap up an affordable city souvenir in Hello Chicago. There is a food hall on the top floor.
🔹 H4 ✉ 700 N Michigan Avenue ☎ 312/266 7710 🚇 Red line: Chicago 🚌 145, 146, 147, 151

THE JEWELER'S CENTER
Jewellery and other related products are sold in more than 140 outlets on 13 floors; if you can't find what you're looking for here, the chances are you never will.
🔹 H6 ✉ 5 S Wabash Avenue ☎ 312/853 2057 🚇 Brown, Orange lines: Madison 🚌 38

MARSHALL FIELD'S
Chicagoans adore this department store, which carries clothing, furnishings and household goods, jewellery, exotic foods, books, and more. There are several branches in Chicago, but this is the parent and the best. The building includes a Tiffany glass dome and an interior design that outdoes Carson Pirie Scott and adds to the aura of glamour. The store's own Frango Mints, sold in the basement Market Place section, make a good souvenir.
🔹 H6 ✉ 111 N State Street ☎ 312/781 1000 🚇 Blue, Red lines: Washington 🚌 6, 11, 29, 36, 44, 62, 146

NAVY PIER
Some 60 shops are gathered in this

complex of restaurants and entertainments. If you're thinking of buying a lot of souvenirs as gifts, this is not a bad place to look.

➕ J5 ✉ 700 E Grand Avenue ☎ 312/595 PIER 🚇 Red line: Grand 🚌 29, 56, 65, 66

NEIMAN-MARCUS

Exclusive, elegant clothing is the forte of Neiman-Marcus, which also boasts a fine range of beauty products and a food market that delights gourmets. Looking around this handsome store is good fun, even if you can't afford to buy the products.

➕ H5 ✉ 737 N Michigan Avenue ☎ 312/642 5900 🚇 Red line: Chicago 🚌 145, 146, 147, 151

900 NORTH MICHIGAN SHOPS

This gleaming marble high-rise consumes an entire city block. Restaurants, cinemas and shops are grouped around a six-storey atrium; a branch of New York's revered Bloomingdale's department store is an anchor. There are also many smaller, speciality stores, including a Gucci outlet and Gallery Lara, where exquisite glass sculptures sell for tens of thousands of dollars.

➕ H4 ✉ 900 N Michigan Avenue ☎ 312/915 3900 🚇 Red line: Chicago 🚌 145, 146, 147, 151

NORTH PIER

Entertaining speciality shops are a dime a dozen in this collection of

shops, snack-stands and various amusements.

➕ J5 ✉ North Pier, 435 E Illinois Street ☎ 312/836 4300 🚇 Red line: Grand 🚌 29, 56, 65, 66

ONE MAGNIFICENT MILE

The perfect place to exceed your credit-card limit. A seemingly endless array of chic designer shops such as Chanel and Polo Ralph Lauren crowds this stylish high-rise building.

➕ H4 ✉ 940–80 N Michigan Avenue ☎ 312/664 7777 🚇 Red line: Chicago 🚌 145, 146, 147, 151

WATER TOWER PLACE

Packing these seven floors are clothing stores for men, women and children, jewellers, art galleries, home-furnishing emporiums and perfumeries. In addition, there are cinemas and restaurants; if you tire, rest beside the indoor shrubbery and miniature waterfalls, or be decadent and treat yourself to some chocolates from Godiva Chocolatier.

➕ H4 ✉ 835 N Michigan Avenue ☎ 312/440 3165 🚇 Red line: Chicago 🚌 145, 146, 147, 151

The making of the Magnificent Mile

No Chicago shopper could be unaware that most top-class stores are gathered along the section of Michigan Avenue known as the Magnificent Mile (➤ 51). Many shops appeared here following the 1920s opening of the river bridge linking Michigan Avenue to the Loop, but the 'Magnificent Mile' concept was a 1940s idea that eventually mutated into today's rows of marble-clad towers, mostly built during the 1970s and 1980s.

CLOTHES

Curious clothing

Should the sensible buying of sensible clothes for sensible everyday wear suddenly become a stultifyingly dull pursuit, you can let your sartorial imaginations run riot at Fantasy Headquarters (✉ 4065 N Milwaukee Avenue). This enormous store carries hundreds of outrageous costumes, masks and assorted outlandish accessories, for sale or rent, for the dresser who dares.

BANANA REPUBLIC
The hugely popular local branch of the nationally known supplier of quality casualwear.
✚ H5 ✉ 744 N Michigan Avenue ☎ 312/642 0020 Ⓡ Red line: Chicago 🚌 145, 146, 147, 151

BARNEYS NEW YORK
The Chicago branch of a Manhattan store noted for chic women's clothing, and for its extensive selection of fine menswear.
✚ H4 ✉ 25 E Oak Street ☎ 312/587 1700 Ⓡ Red line: Chicago 🚌 145, 146, 147, 151

BROOKS BROTHERS
Well-made attire for men, in conservative styles, plus some equally stodgy clothing for women.
✚ H5 ✉ 713 N Michigan Avenue ☎ 312/915 0060 Ⓡ Red line: Chicago 🚌 145, 146, 147, 151

COUNTY SEAT
Stocks Levi jeans in all conceivable sizes and styles; and regularly marks down certain lines.
✚ H4 ✉ 835 N Michigan Avenue ☎ 312/664 7837 Ⓡ Red line: Chicago 🚌 145, 146, 147, 151

J CREW
Classic modern clothes, shoes and accessories for men and women. Businesswomen come here for choice officewear.
✚ H4 ✉ 900 N Michigan Avenue ☎ 312/751 2739 Ⓡ Red line: Chicago 🚌 145, 146, 147, 151

GIANNI VERSACE
The Midwest flagship store of the inventive and pricey designer.
✚ H4 ✉ 101 E Oak Street ☎ 312/337 1111 Ⓡ Red line: Chicago 🚌 145, 146, 147, 151

LORD & TAYLOR
One of the stores in the Water Tower Place vertical mall. Up-market clothes, shoes and accessories for men and women.
✚ H4 ✉ Water Tower Place, 835 N Michigan Avenue ☎ 312/787 7400 Ⓡ Red line: Chicago 🚌 145, 146, 147, 151

PETITE SOPHISTICATE
An impressive assortment of stylish business and leisure clothing aimed at the smaller-than-average woman.
✚ H4 ✉ 700 N Michigan Avenue ☎ 312/787 4923 Ⓡ Red line: Chicago 🚌 145, 146, 147, 151

SULKA
For the man with money, this is the place to be fitted out in a fine-quality handmade suit; men without money might ogle at the hand-crafted silk ties.
✚ H4 ✉ 55 E Oak Street ☎ 312/951 9500 Ⓡ Red line: Chicago 🚌 145, 146, 147, 151

ULTIMO
Where the glamorous woman about town picks up her latest designer wear. Top names are represented here; the clothes are fabulous and so are the prices.
✚ H4 ✉ 114 E Oak Street ☎ 312/787 0906 Ⓡ Red line: Chicago 🚌 145, 146, 147, 151

ACCESSORIES & VINTAGE CLOTHES

FLASHY TRASH
Chicago's major trove of vintage clothing, ranging from Victorian evening wear to garish 1970s disco duds.
Off map ✉ 3524 N Halsted Street ☎ 773/327 6900 Red line: Addison ▤ 152

GLOVE ME TENDER
Every kind of hand covering that a man, woman or child could ever want.
H4 ✉ 920 N Michigan Avenue ☎ 312/664 4022 Red line: Chicago ▤ 145, 146, 147, 151

HERMÈS OF PARIS
Chicago branch of the Parisian fashion house, and a certainty for lovely scarves, handbags, ties and leather items.
H4 ✉ 110 E Oak Street ☎ 312/787 8175 Red line: Chicago ▤ 145, 146, 147, 151

HOLLYWOOD MIRROR
Two floors packed with colourful garb of recent decades, mostly women's apparel but also menswear, and a collection of lamps, jewellery and oddities. The stock has been sorted – unlike the clothes at Ragstock, upstairs – so prices are higher.
Off map ✉ 812 W Belmont Street ☎ 773/404 4510 Brown, Red lines: Belmont ▤ 77

HUBBA-HUBBA
Great vintage dresses, blouses and jewellery for women, and 1950s suits and sweaters for men.
Off map ✉ 3338 N Clark Street ☎ 773/477 1414

Brown, Red lines: Belmont ▤ 22

RAGSTOCK
The quantity of used clothing is huge, and prices are very low. It takes time to sort through the dross, but you might find a great bargain. Upstairs from Hollywood Mirror.
Off map ✉ 812 N Belmont Street ☎ 773/868 9263 Brown, Red lines: Belmont ▤ 77

SILVER MOON
Bargains are few but quality is everywhere at this sizeable emporium of vintage clothing. Look for immaculate evening wear from the roaring 1920s.
Off map ✉ 3337 N Halsted Street ☎ 773/883 0222 Red line: Addison ▤ 152

TIFFANY & CO
The celebrated New York jeweller offers a scintillating assortment of stones, plus superb watches, crystal, china and more.
H4 ✉ 715 N Michigan Avenue ☎ 312/944 7500 Red line: Chicago ▤ 145, 146, 147, 151

URBAN OUTFITTERS
The hippest accessories, to match the store's up-to-the-minute clothes, plus funky items for the home.
H4 ✉ 935 E Walton Street ☎ 312/640 1919 Red Line: Chicago ▤ 145, 146, 147, 151

Tender buttons
At Tender Buttons (✉ 946 N Rush Street) the thousands of buttons in thousands of styles on sale are displayed with a museum-like reverence, and are complemented by a fine selection of Edwardian cufflinks.

ART, ANTIQUES & COLLECTABLES

Collectables from far corners

Artworks and other items from the far-flung corners of the globe are the stock-in-trade of two Chicago stores. Primitive Art Works (706 N Wells Street) sells tribal and cultural art, as well as artefacts from Africa, the South Pacific, Indonesia, and Central and South America. The Alaska Shop (104 E Oak Street) stocks works created by the Inuit people of Alaska, Canada and Siberia.

CITY OF CHICAGO STORE

Though the main stock is new merchandise from city cultural institutions, the store also has a quirky range of restored items – traffic lights, ballot boxes, parking meters and so on – gathered together from Chicago's streets and administrative offices.

J5 North Pier, 401 E Illinois Street 312/467 1111 Red line: Grand 29, 56, 65, 66

FLY BY NITE GALLERY

A clutter of art deco jewellery and ceramics, and more *objets d'art* than you can shake a stick at.

G5 714 N Wells Street 312/664 8136 Brown line: Chicago 37, 41

JAY ROBERT'S ANTIQUE WAREHOUSE

You'll find everything from clocks to fireplaces among the antiques and junk that fill a massive 50,000sq ft of floor space here.

G5 149 W Kinzie Street 312/222 0167 Brown, Purple lines: Merchandise Mart 36, 62

POSTER PLUS

A good assortment of historic posters, mostly celebrating landmarks in Chicago and US history, though many are attractive reprints rather than originals.

H7 200 S Michigan Avenue 312/461 9277 Brown, Orange lines: Adams 3, 4, 6, 38

R H LOVE GALLERIES

Housed in a 19th-century mansion, the extensive and expensive selection of American art from all eras is particularly strong on Impressionists.

H5 40 E Erie Street 312/640 1300 Red line: Chicago, Grand 22, 36

STEVE STARR STUDIOS

A wonderful stock of original art deco paraphernalia, ranging from silver cigarette cases to chrome cocktail shakers.

E1 2779 N Lincoln Avenue 773/525 6530 Brown line: Diversey 11, 76

VINTAGE POSTERS INTERNATIONAL

Stylish posters from the US and Europe, dating from the 1880s, plus a diverse selection of French decorative items of the *belle époque*.

G3 1551 N Wells Street 312/951 6681 Brown line: Sedgwick 135, 156

WRIGLEYVILLE ANTIQUE MALL

Absorbing stock of kitsch household items, from furniture to ornaments, mostly dating from the 1950s and 1960s.

Off map 3336 N Clark Street 773/868 0285 Brown, Red lines: Belmont 22

BOOKS

BARBARA'S BOOKSTORE

Old, new and otherwise hard-to-find literature, plus political and contemporary lifestyle titles.

✚ G3 ✉ 1350 N Wells Street ☎ 312/642 5044 🚇 Brown line: Sedgwick. Red line: Clark/Division 🚌 11, 156

BORDERS BOOKS & MUSIC

A large selection of titles, plus a café.

✚ H4 ✉ 830 N Michigan Avenue ☎ 312/573 0564 🚇 Red line: Chicago 🚌 145, 146, 147, 151

CHICAGO ARCHITECTURE FOUNDATION

Exemplary source of books on architecture.

✚ H7 ✉ 224 S Michigan Avenue ☎ 312/922 3432 🚇 Brown, Orange lines: Adams 🚌 3, 4, 6, 38

57TH STREET BOOKS

One of Hyde Park's long-serving bookshops with both new and used volumes. Toys are provided for children of browsing parents.

✚ Off map ✉ 5757 S University Avenue ☎ 773/752 4381 🚇 Red line: Garfield 🚌 1, 4, 28, 51 🚆 55th, 56th, 57th Street

RAIN DOG BOOKS

Antiquarian and rare titles.

✚ H7 ✉ 404 S Michigan Avenue ☎ 312/922 1200 🚇 Red line: Harrison 🚌 1, 7, 126

RAND MCNALLY MAP STORE

Atlases, regional and city street maps; guidebooks.

✚ H5 ✉ 444 N Michigan Avenue ☎ 312/321 1751 🚇 Red line: Grand 🚌 3, 11, 145, 146, 147, 151

RIZZOLI BOOKSTORE

Large stock of general books, and a strong selection on art, architecture and music.

✚ H4 ✉ 835 N Michigan Avenue ☎ 312/642 3500 🚇 Red line: Chicago 🚌 145, 146, 147, 151

THE STARS OUR DESTINATION

Science fiction, fantasy and horror; new and second-hand tomes.

✚ Off map ✉ 1021 W Belmont Avenue ☎ 773/871 2722 🚇 Brown, Red lines: Belmont 🚌 77

STUART BRENT

A Chicago institution, well stocked with general titles, plus art and music books.

✚ G6 ✉ 309 W Washington Street ☎ 312/364 0126 🚇 Red line: Grand 🚌 3, 11, 145, 146, 147, 151

UNABRIDGED BOOKSTORE

Titles of particular interest to gays and lesbians, plus general stock.

✚ Off map ✉ 3251 N Broadway ☎ 773/883 9119 🚇 Brown, Red lines: Belmont 🚌 136

WOMEN & CHILDREN FIRST

Books primarily aimed at women, plus fiction and children's titles.

✚ Off map ✉ 5233 N Clark Street ☎ 773/769 9299 🚇 Red line: Berwyn 🚌 22

Printer's Row bookshops

A cluster of noteworthy bookshops lies just south of the Loop in Printer's Row (➤ 51). Among them are Prairie Avenue Bookshop (✉ 418 S Wabash Avenue), with seemingly every tome on architecture and town planning ever published; Sandmeyer's Bookstore (✉ 714 S Dearborn Street), strong on travel titles; and Powell's Bookstore (✉ 828 S Wabash Avenue), which carries second-hand books on all subjects.

Barnes & Noble in Chicago

This branch of the nationwide chain (✚ F1 ✉ 659 W Diversey Parkway ☎ 773/871 9004 🚇 Brown line: Diversey 🚌 22, 36, 76) is a superstore, offering extensive shelves of general titles, newspapers and magazines, and an atmosphere conducive to browsing. There is also a café.

DISCOUNT, CATALOGUE & FACTORY STORES

Long-distance discount shopping

Two major outlet malls on the edge of the Chicago area are worth the trip. An hour or so's journey west finds Gurnee Mills (☎ 800/937 7467), whose 200-plus stores are easily combined with a trip to Six Flags Great America (► 21). An hour south in Michigan City, Indiana, is Lighthouse Place (☎ 800/866 5900), another extensive group of factory retail outlets.

BUY-A-TUX

A huge stock of men's formal wear made affordable, with up to 40 per cent off normal retail prices; it also carries discounted evening wear for women and children.

✚ F8 ✉ 615 W Roosevelt Road ☎ 312/243 5465 🚇 Red line: Roosevelt 🚌 12

CRATE & BARREL OUTLET

A small factory outlet with hefty discounts on the admirable Crate & Barrel range of houseware, furniture and various home accessories.

✚ F3 ✉ 800 W North Avenue ☎ 312/787 4775 🚇 Brown line: Sedgwick

DESIGNER RESALE

Names such as Armani and Chanel are among the designer labels offered second-hand in this chic womenswear boutique.

✚ G5 ✉ 658 N Dearborn Street ☎ 312/587 3312 🚇 Red line: Grand 🚌 22

FILENE'S BASEMENT

Sort through the formidably large stock – spread over several floors – for brand-name and designer clothing and accessories, for men and women, mostly at prices 30–60 per cent lower than retail.

✚ H4 ✉ 830 N Michigan Avenue ☎ 312/482 8918 🚇 Red line: Chicago 🚌 145, 146, 147, 151
Also at:
✚ G6 ✉ 1 N State Street

FOX'S

Recent and current top-name designer clothing for women – for business, sport and casual wear – at discounted prices.

✚ F1 ✉ 2336 N Clark Street ☎ 773/281 0700 🚇 Brown line: Fullerton 🚌 22, 36

GAP FACTORY OUTLET

Big discounts on stock from Gap and Banana Republic.

✚ B/C2 ✉ 2778 N Milwaukee Avenue ☎ 773/252 0594 🚇 Western

MCSHANE'S EXCHANGE

The latest designer clothing for women, barely worn and temptingly priced, plus a wide selection of accessories.

✚ F2 ✉ 815 W Armitage Avenue ☎ 773/525 0282 🚇 Brown line: Armitage 🚌 73

THE SECOND CHILD

Designer-name children's clothes, furnishings, toys and more, second-hand but rarely in less than excellent condition.

✚ E2 ✉ 954 W Armitage Avenue ☎ 773/883 0880 🚇 Brown line: Armitage 🚌 73

SUIT EXCHANGE

Enormous collections of new and previously worn suits, among them designer names at rock-bottom prices.

✚ H6 ✉ 115 N Wabash Avenue ☎ 312/236 5880 🚇 Blue, Red lines: Washington 🚌 6, 11, 29, 36, 44, 62, 146

MISCELLANEOUS

THE ARCHITECTURAL REVOLUTION
Chicago's best collection of garden gnomes amid pseudo-Roman columns and other wacky decorative items.
➕ Off map ✉ 856 W Belmont Avenue ☎ 312/752 7837 🚇 Brown, Red lines: Belmont

CENTRAL CAMERA COMPANY
A long-established photographers' shop, with a large stock of new and second-hand cameras and equipment.
➕ H7 ✉ 232 S Wabash Avenue ☎ 312/427 5580 🚇 Brown, Orange lines: Adams 🚌 1, 7, 60, 126

CHICAGO MUSIC MART
Pianos, *okavina* and Indian *tablas* are among the instruments offered by this gathering of music retailers; if the prices are beyond your means, console yourself with musically themed sweets.
➕ H7 ✉ 333 S State Street ☎ 312/362 6700 🚇 Blue, Red lines: Jackson 🚌 1, 7, 60, 126, 145, 146, 147, 151

CRATE & BARREL
Stylish and reasonably priced kitchenware, furniture and household accessories. For the Crate & Barrel factory outlet, ➤ 76.
➕ H5 ✉ 646 N Michigan Avenue ☎ 312/787 5900 🚇 Red line: Chicago 🚌 145, 146, 147, 151
Also at:
➕ H6 ✉ 101 N Wabash Avenue ☎ 312/372 0100 🚇 Blue, Red lines: Washington

JAZZ RECORD MART
Mainstream releases and cult rarities are among thousands of CDs, records and tapes.
➕ G5 ✉ 11 W Grand Avenue ☎ 312/222 1467 🚇 Red line: Grand 🚌 29, 65

NIKE TOWN
Even if you couldn't care less about Nike sportswear, a visit to this pulsating, themed, tri-level store – complete with aquarium – is a must.
➕ H5 ✉ 669 N Michigan Avenue ☎ 312/642 6363 🚇 Red line: Chicago 🚌 145, 146, 147, 151

THE SAVVY TRAVELLER
Everything travellers might need – even if they do not realise it before they come here – from money belts to guidebooks.
➕ H7 ✉ 310 S Michigan Avenue ☎ 312/913 9800 🚇 Brown, Orange lines: Adams 🚌 3, 4, 6, 38

TOWER RECORDS
Every record or CD ever released in any musical category (it seems), plus a large selection of books and videos.
➕ G2 ✉ 2301 N Clark Street ☎ 773/477 5994 🚇 Brown, Red lines: Fullerton 🚌 22, 36

TREASURE ISLAND
Shop here for a luxury picnic or edible gift. There are several branches of this gourmet supermarket.
➕ G4 ✉ 75 W Elm Street ☎ 312/440 1144 🚇 Red line: Clark/Division 🚌 36, 70

Cigars and more
Chicago has several stores for the discerning smoker: all offer quality, hand-rolled cigars and most also have selections of imported cigarettes and smokers' accessories. Three of the best are Around the World Tobacco (✉ 1044 W Belmont Avenue), The Cigar Spot (✉ Biggsy & Curruthers, 605 N Michigan Avenue) and Little Havana (✉ 6 W Maple Street and at Navy Pier, ➤ 60).

77

BLUES & JAZZ VENUES

Grant Park's blues and jazz

Each June and September the Petrillo Music Shell in Grant Park (► 41) is the stage for blues and jazz festivals respectively, which draw top international names as well as the city's greats in both fields. The performers are greeted by tens of thousands of their admirers, who arrive with blankets and picnic supplies to enjoy the free music.

ANDY'S LOUNGE

Popular and unpretentious jazz venue that earns its keep by staging commendable sets on weekday lunchtimes, as well as early and mid-evening shows.

✚ H5 ✉ 11 E Hubbard Street ☎ 312/642 6805 🚇 Red line: Grand 🚌 29, 36

B.L.U.E.S.

Small, dimly lit, but very atmospheric spot to hear some of the best blues artists around, including some legendary old-timers.

✚ F1 ✉ 2519 N Halsted Street ☎ 773/528 1012 🚇 Brown, Red lines: Fullerton 🚌 8

B.L.U.E.S. ETCETERA

This offshoot of B.L.U.E.S. is slightly larger than its progenitor and just as dependable.

✚ Off map ✉ 1124 W Belmont ☎ 773/525 8989 🚇 Brown, Red lines: Belmont 🚌 77

BOP SHOP

An intimate venue often featuring some of the pick of Chicago's home-grown jazz talent, playing to a relaxed but knowledgeable neighbourhood crowd.

✚ D4 ✉ 1807 W Division Street ☎ 773/235 3232 🚇 Blue line: Division 🚌 70

BUDDY GUY'S LEGENDS

Co-owner and famed blues guitarist Buddy Guy presents outstanding blues acts, including internationally known names and Chicago's own rising stars.

✚ H7 ✉ 754 S Wabash Avenue ☎ 312/427 0333 🚇 Red line: Harrison 🚌 12

THE BULLS

The archetypal smoke-filled jazz club – rough on the lungs, but the sounds are great.

✚ G2 ✉ 1916 N Lincoln Park West ☎ 312/337 3000 🚇 Brown line: Sedgwick 🚌 156

DICK'S LAST RESORT

A great place to hear Dixieland jazz if you don't mind noisy crowds.

✚ J5 ✉ North Pier, 435 E Illinois Street ☎ 312/836 7870 🚇 Red line: Grand 🚌 29, 56, 65, 66

GREEN MILL

Well north of the city centre in an unfashionable area, but worth the journey for jazz that is always good, sometimes brilliant. On Sunday nights, poets take the stage for competitive poetry reading – more entertaining than you might think.

✚ F1 ✉ 4802 N Broadway ☎ 773/878 5552 🚇 Brown line: Diversey

NEW CHECKERBOARD LOUNGE

One of the legendary venues of Chicago's South Side blues scene is still an exciting spot for some of the city's best blues, played to a racially mixed crowd. Plan on taking a taxi to and from your hotel.

✚ Off map ✉ 1634 W 69th Street ☎ 773/471 53000 🚇 Red line: 47th Street 🚌 43

COMEDY, FOLK, ROCK & REGGAE VENUES

ALL JOKES ASIDE
Quality comedians
throughout the week
and an 'open-mike'
night on Wednesdays.
✚ H8 ✉ 1000 Wabash
Avenue ☎ 312/922 0577
Ⓖ Orange line: Roosevelt
🚌 12

CUBBY BEAR LOUNGE
The live music at this
sports bar opposite
Wrigley Field spans
rock, country, reggae
and blues. Dancing
and beer.
✚ Off map ✉ 1059 W
Addison Street ☎ 773/327
1662 Ⓖ Brown line: Addison
🚌 22, 152

ELBO ROOM
Innovative spot for live
alternative rock music,
often featuring the
hottest new acts, plus
regular poetry readings
and comedy.
✚ Off map ✉ 2871 N Lincoln
Avenue ☎ 773/549 5549
Ⓖ Brown line: Diversey 🚌 11

HOT HOUSE
Trendy, warehouse-like
spot in Wicker Park,
with eclectic music and
an arty crowd.
✚ C/D2/3 ✉ 2234 W Medill
Avenue ☎ 773/235 2334
Ⓖ Damen

KITTY O'SHEA'S
Ersatz Irish pub with
real Irish music,
re-created inside the
Chicago Hilton and
Towers hotel.
✚ H7 ✉ 720 S Michigan
Avenue ☎ 800/HILTONS or
312/922 4400 Ⓖ Red line:
Harrison 🚌 1, 3, 4, 6, 146

LOUNGE AX
Bar-like venue,
showcasing the rising
names in alternative and
indie rock. Bigger names
bring huge crowds.
✚ F1 ✉ 2438 N Lincoln
Avenue ☎ 773/525 6620
Ⓖ Brown, Red lines: Fullerton
🚌 11

METRO
The city's major mid-
sized venue for live rock
music, with ample space
for dancing and plentiful
seating with good views.
Other levels have a
nightclub and a coffee
bar.
✚ Off map ✉ 3730 N Clark
Street ☎ 773/549 0203
Ⓖ Brown line: Addison 🚌 22,
152

**OLD TOWN SCHOOL
OF FOLK MUSIC**
This institution is
dedicated to the study
of folk music, and
usually has two nightly
shows from leading
folksters.
✚ E2 ✉ 909 W Armitage
Avenue ☎ 773/525 7793
Ⓖ Brown line: Armitage 🚌 73

**THE WILD HARE &
SINGING ARMADILLO
FROG SANCTUARY**
Top-notch live reggae
and occasionally other
Caribbean and African
sounds.
✚ Off map ✉ 3530 N Clark
Street ☎ 773/327 4273
Ⓖ Brown line: Addison 🚌 22,
152

ZANIES
Small and enjoyable
comedy club, featuring
rising local stars as well
as better-known names.
✚ G3 ✉ 1548 N Wells Street
☎ 312/337 4027 Ⓖ Brown
line: Sedgwick 🚌 11, 156

Showtimes

Most comedy clubs open nightly,
sometimes with two shows per
night; the busiest nights (usually
with the biggest names) are
Friday and Saturday, when
booking is essential. As a rule,
mid-sized live music venues
open around 8PM or 9PM. The
main act usually ends by
midnight, although drinking
and dancing might continue
into the small hours.

CLASSICAL MUSIC, THEATRE & THE PERFORMING ARTS

Ravinia Festival

From mid-June to Labor Day, the northern suburb of Highland Park plays host to the Ravinia Festival. The summer home of the Chicago Symphony Orchestra, Ravinia also stages rock and jazz concerts, dance events, and other cultural activities. Chartered buses ferry festival-goers the 25 miles from central Chicago; you can also get there by commuter train. For further details:
☎ 312/RAVINIA.

ANNOYANCE THEATER
Searing comedy and spoofs, much of it developed from improvised sketches; audience participation is encouraged.
✛ Off map ✉ 3747 N Clark Street ☎ 773/929 6200 🚇 Red line: Addison 🚌 36

AUDITORIUM THEATER
Designed by the revered Adler & Sullivan partnership, the Auditorium Building, which holds the theatre, was the world's heaviest when completed in 1889. The marvellously renovated historic theatre has excellent acoustics and sightlines, and makes a fitting venue for prestigious dance, music and drama productions.
✛ H7 ✉ 50 E Congress Parkway ☎ 312/922 2110 🚇 Red line: Harrison 🚌 6, 145, 146, 147, 151

CANDLELIT DINNER PLAYHOUSE
There are few surprises in the material here – the shows are usually classic Broadway musicals, very well done. You can get a reasonably priced dinner-and-theatre deal, or go for entertainment alone. The theatre is just outside Chicago.
✛ Off map ✉ 5620 Harlem Avenue, Summit ☎ 708/496 3000

CHICAGO THEATER
Broadway blockbusters, local shows and star-studded musical events

grace the stage, though an equal attraction is the building itself – an ornate 1920s movie palace, now restored.
✛ G6 ✉ 175 N State Street ☎ 312/443 1130 🚇 Red line: Washington 🚌 6, 11, 29, 36, 44, 62, 145, 146

CIVIC OPERA HOUSE
The highly regarded Lyric Opera of Chicago company performs from mid-September to early February at this art deco auditorium. Although most seats are sold through annual subscription, a few are sometimes available at the box office on the day of performance. This is also one of the main dance performance spaces in the city.
✛ G6 ✉ 20 N Wacker Drive ☎ 312/332 2244 🚇 Brown, Orange lines: Madison/Wells 🚌 129

GOODMAN THEATER
Adjoining the Art Institute of Chicago (► 40), the Goodman Theater hosts some of the best drama in the city, including both classics and cutting-edge contemporary productions. The latter are often staged in the smaller of the building's two auditoriums.
✛ H6 ✉ 200 S Columbus Drive ☎ 312/443 3800 🚇 Brown, Orange lines: Adams 🚌 3, 4, 60, 145, 147, 151

LUNAR CABARET AND FULL MOON CAFÉ
An inviting, low-key setting for an enterprising programme

of classical performances by small ensembles, usually on weekends.

✚ Off map ✉ 2827 N Lincoln Avenue ☎ 773/327 6666 Ⓡ Brown line: Diversey 🚌 11

MERLE RESKIN THEATRE

A French Renaissance-style building of 1910 that houses diverse operatic, dance and musical events, often featuring up-and-coming local and student talent.

✚ H7 ✉ 60 E Balbo Avenue ☎ 773/325 7900 Ⓡ Red line: Harrison 🚌 12

ORCHESTRA HALL

This sumptuous Greek Revival hall, built in 1904, is the home of the renowned Chicago Symphony Orchestra (CSO), which is in residence from September to May. Although tickets are snapped up early, some are available on the day of performance; call the box office for details. The Civic Orchestra of Chicago (a training orchestra that often gives free concerts) and the Chicago Symphony Orchestra Chorus also appear here.

✚ H7 ✉ 220 S Michigan Avenue ☎ 312/294 3000 Ⓡ Brown, Orange lines: Adams 🚌 1, 3, 4, 6, 7, 38, 60

THE SECOND CITY

Biting satire and inspired improvisation have long been the stock-in-trade here, and they have been so successful that a second Second City theatre has grown up next door. It

offers a different show simultaneously.

✚ G3 ✉ 1616 N Wells Street ☎ 773/642 8189 Ⓡ Brown line: Sedgwick 🚌 11, 156

SHUBERT THEATER

Dating back to the 19th century, the handsome Shubert is a rare reminder that theatre once thrived in the Loop. Dance companies perform here, though it is not exclusively a dance theatre. It is best known for its musicals.

✚ G6 ✉ 22 W Madison Street ☎ 312/902 1500 Ⓡ Brown, Orange lines: Madison/Wells

STEPPENWOLF THEATER

Home of the enormously successful and influential Steppenwolf repertory company, founded in 1976, and still a premier venue for the best of Off-Loop theatre. The theatre has a 900-seat main hall and a smaller space where experimental drama is produced.

✚ F3 ✉ 1650 N Halsted Street ☎ 312/335 1650 Ⓡ Red line: North/Clybourn 🚌 8, 72

VICTORY GARDENS THEATER

Founded in 1974, the Victory Gardens Theater provides performance space for the works of aspiring but overlooked Chicago-based playwrights.

✚ F2 ✉ 2257 N Lincoln Avenue ☎ 312/871 3000 Ⓡ Brown, Red lines: Fullerton 🚌 11

Half-price theatre tickets

Hot Tix (✉ 108 N State Street) offers half-price tickets for many of the day's theatre events. Another convenient branch is at Chicago Place (Level 6), 700 N Michigan Avenue. A recorded message (☎ 312/977 1755) lists the day's performances. Full-price advance tickets are also available from Hot Tix, and from another agency, Ticketmaster (☎ 312/559 1212 to charge by phone, or ☎ 312/559 8989 for information).

Comedy shows

Two comedy shows have been entertaining Chicago theatre-goers for years. *Tony 'n' Tina's Wedding* (✉ 230 W North Avenue ☎ 312/664 8844), which started out in New York, re-creates an Italian-American wedding; the performers mingle with the audience ('the guests'). Meanwhile, *Shear Madness* (✉ Mayfair Theatre, Blackstone Hotel, 636 S Michigan Avenue ☎ 312/786 9120) is a comedy 'whodunit' set in a hairdressing salon; the jokes are regularly updated and audience participation is encouraged.

NIGHTCLUBS

Nightclub news

The most general source is the Friday edition of the *Chicago Tribune*. Inside info on the latest clubs, as well as the nightlife scene in general, can be found in the pages of the weekly *Chicago Reader* and *New City*, both free. Also weekly and free is the *Windy City Times*, which carries details of nightlife for gays and lesbians.

ASI ES COLOMBIA
Open only on weekends, this salsa club puts on good bands and attracts good dancers.
✚ Off map ✉ 3910 N Lincoln Avenue ☎ 773/348 7444 🚇 Brown line: Diversey 🚌 11

BAJA BEACH CLUB
Dancing, plus live, varied music and video games are all part of the attraction in this generally crowded venue.
✚ J5 ✉ North Pier, 401 E Illinois Street ☎ 312/222 1993 🚇 Red line: Grand 🚌 29, 56, 65, 66

BERLIN
A big and immensely popular gay and lesbian nightspot, Berlin puts on themed nights throughout the week (phone for details). Draws a mixed crowd, and packed to bursting on Fridays and Saturdays.
✚ Off map ✉ 954 W Belmont Avenue ☎ 773/348 4975 🚇 Brown, Red lines: Belmont 🚌 77

DRINK
A riotous restaurant and bar in the former meatpacking district that later transforms into a dance venue featuring throbbing live music. Particularly popular with dealers from the nearby financial institutions.
✚ F6 ✉ 702 W Fulton Street ☎ 312/733 7300 🚌 56

EXCALIBUR
This complex of billiards, pinball and video games, plus discos and a restaurant – all incongruously set in a 19th-century pseudo-Gothic castle – is a favourite with twenty-somethings. The sturdy granite structure was built in the 1890s as the second home of the Chicago Historical Society.
✚ G5 ✉ 632 N Dearborn Street ☎ 312/266 1944 🚇 Red line: Grand 🚌 22

JILLY'S RETRO CLUB
Being dressed smartly and aged 25 or over are prerequisites for entry to Jilly's; being rich helps too, as does a belief that the disco sounds of the 1970s were dance music's finest moments.
✚ H4 ✉ 1009 N Rush Street ☎ 733/664 1001 🚇 Red line: Chicago 🚌 36

NEO
An ultra-cool crowd laps up sounds ranging from industrial dance and techno to (slightly) more mainstream music. By city nightlife standards, this is an old-timer of a venue.
✚ G2 ✉ 2350 N Clark Street ☎ 773/528 2622 🚇 Brown, Red lines: Fullerton 🚌 22, 36

BARS

BILLY GOAT TAVERN
This below-street-level watering hole is a favourite among local journalists, but appeals to anyone in search of a simple, unpretentious place to drink.

⊞ H5 ✉ 430 N Michigan Avenue ☎ 312/222 1525 🚇 Red line: Grand 🚌 145, 146, 147, 151

COQ D'OR
Buddy Charles presides at this piano bar in the Drake Hotel.

⊞ H4 ✉ 140 E Walton Place ☎ 800/5 DRAKE or 312/787 2200 🚇 Red line: Chicago 🚌 145, 146, 147, 151

GAMEKEEPERS TAVERN & GRILL
A rowdy sports bar packed with televisions and raucous, twenty-something drinkers.

⊞ G2 ✉ 1971 N Lincoln Avenue ☎ 773/549 0400 🚇 Brown line: Armitage 🚌 11

HARRY CARAY'S
Created, and named after, the legendary Chicago Cubs broadcaster who died in 1998, this sports bar is packed with baseball memorabilia. It's a great place to be after a Cubs win, and the Italian food is good, too.

⊞ G5 ✉ 33 W Kinzie Street ☎ 312/465 9269 🚇 Red line: Grand 🚌 62

HOUSE OF BEER
A promising selection of microbrewery beers from around the US, in an ersatz fishing shack.

⊞ G4 ✉ 16 W Division Street ☎ 312/642 2344 🚇 Red line: Clark/Division 🚌 36, 70

JOHN BARLEYCORN MEMORIAL PUB
Established in the 1890s, this sizeable pub not only slakes the thirst but provides classical music and a continuous slide show of great works of art.

⊞ F2 ✉ 658 W Belden Avenue ☎ 773/348 8899 🚇 Brown, Red lines: Fullerton 🚌 11

OLD TOWN ALEHOUSE
Downbeat drinking den of long standing. The diverse jukebox sounds are as eclectic as the widely varied clientele.

⊞ G3 ✉ 219 W North Avenue ☎ 312/944 7020 🚇 Brown line: Sedgwick 🚌 72

POPS FOR CHAMPAGNE
A well-heeled and well-dressed crowd selects from a big choice of champagnes in a stylish setting. You can get a light meal here, and listen to live jazz.

⊞ Off map ✉ 2934 N Sheffield Avenue ☎ 312/472 1000 🚇 Brown line: Wellington 🚌 8

WEEDS
Welcoming, anything-goes bar catering for artists, poets, misfits, and those who like drinking with them.

⊞ F3 ✉ 1555 N Dayton Street ☎ 312/943 7815 🚇 Red line: North/Clybourn 🚌 8

ZEBRA LOUNGE
An intimate, characterful piano bar with a loyal following, the Zebra is open late most nights.

⊞ G/H4 ✉ 1220 N State Street ☎ 312/642 5140 🚇 Red line: Chicago 🚌 36

Liquor laws
Some bars serve alcohol until 2AM every night except Saturday, when they may do so until 3AM on Sunday morning. Others continue serving until 4AM (5AM on Sunday mornings). Alcohol may be served only to persons aged 21 or over; ID may well be required from anyone who looks under age. Shops may not sell alcohol before noon on Sundays.

LUXURY HOTELS

Prices and discounts

The following rates per room are based on two people sharing on a weekday night:

Luxury – over $190

Mid-price – between $100 and $190

Budget – under $100

Many Chicago hotels offer weekend discounts, typically reducing the above prices by 20–40 per cent.

Hostels – $13 per person

Booking

Rooms can be reserved by phone, fax or mail; book as early as possible. A deposit (usually by credit card) equivalent to the nightly rate, will ensure your room is held at least until 6PM; inform the hotel if you are arriving later. Credit card is the usual payment method; travellers' cheques or cash can be used but payment might then be expected in advance. The total charge will include the city's 14.9 per cent sales and room tax.

CHICAGO HILTON & TOWERS
Over 1,500 rooms and a pervasive sense of grandeur. Has the city's largest hotel health club.
⊞ H7 ✉ 720 S Michigan Avenue ☎ 800/HILTONS or 312/922 4400 ¶ Several restaurants (££–£££) ⊞ Red line: Harrison ⊟ 1, 3, 4, 6, 146

THE DRAKE
Modelled on an Italian Renaissance palace, and opened in 1920, this has always been among Chicago's finest hotels. Fabulous lake views.
⊞ H4 ✉ 140 E Walton Place ☎ 800/5 DRAKE or 312/787 2200 ¶ Several restaurants (££–£££) ⊞ Red line: Chicago ⊟ 145, 146, 147, 151

FAIRMONT HOTEL
Winning views over Grant Park, the city centre and the lake; rooms comfortable and tasteful. No health club, but you get a discount at a neighbouring facility.
⊞ H6 ✉ 200 N Columbus Drive ☎ 800/527 4727 or 312/565 8000 ¶ Three good restaurants (££–£££) ⊞ Brown, Orange lines: State, Lake ⊟ 4

FOUR SEASONS
Excellent service, and plush, traditional rooms. Rooftop running track.
⊞ H4 ✉ 120 E Delaware Place ☎ 800/332 3442 or 312/280 8800 ¶ Excellent restaurant (£££) and very good café (££) ⊞ Red line: Chicago ⊟ 145, 146, 147, 151

HYATT ON PRINTER'S ROW
Small and stylish; set within two historic buildings.
⊞ G7 ✉ 500 S Dearborn Street ☎ 800/233 1234 or 312/986 1234 ¶ Excellent restaurant (£££) ⊞ Red line: Harrison ⊟ 24, 36

HOTEL NIKKO
Overlooking the Chicago River, and with every amenity.
⊞ G6 ✉ 320 N Dearborn Street ☎ 800/NIKKO-US or 312/744 1900 ¶ Excellent restaurant (£££) and very good café (££) ⊞ Brown, Orange lines: State ⊟ 62

RENAISSANCE CHICAGO
The convenient Loop location and the spacious, well-equipped rooms make this a good choice for business travellers. Large lobby and lounge.
⊞ H6 ✉ 1 W Wacker Drive ☎ 800/468 3571 or 312/372 7000 ¶ Several good restaurants (££–£££) ⊞ Red line: Lake, State. Brown, Green lines: State ⊟ 2, 10, 11, 44

RITZ-CARLTON
State-of-the-art luxury above a chic mall.
⊞ H5 ✉ 160 E Pearson Street ☎ 800/621 6906 or 312/266 1000 ¶ Several restaurants (££–£££) ⊞ Red line: Chicago ⊟ 157

THE WHITEHALL
First opened in the 1920s. It now has English-style furnishings, and two-line phone and fax machines.
⊞ H4 ✉ 105 E Delaware Place ☎ 800/948 4255 or 312/944 6300 ¶ Excellent restaurant (£££) ⊞ Red line: Chicago ⊟ Any on N Michigan Avenue

MID-PRICE HOTELS

THE ALLEGRO
Easily the best-priced rooms in the Loop. Book well ahead.
🏠 G6 ✉ 171 W Randolph Street ☎ 800/643 1500 or 312/236 0123 🚇 Brown, Orange lines: Randolph/Wells 🚌 37

THE BLACKSTONE
Ageing but elegant, and close to Grant Park. Several presidents have stayed here.
🏠 H7 ✉ 636 S Michigan Avenue ☎ 800/622 6330 or 312/427 4300 🚇 Red line: Harrison 🚌 1, 3, 4, 6, 146

CASS HOTEL
Clean rooms at a great price – but few frills – on the edge of the Magnificent Mile.
🏠 H5 ✉ 640 N Wabash Avenue ☎ 800/227 7850 🚇 Red line: Grand 🚌 29, 65

CITY SUITES HOTEL
Most accommodations are suites, and good value. A lively (if occasionally noisy) shopping and nightlife strip is on the doorstep.
🏠 Off map ✉ 933 W Belmont Avenue ☎ 733/404 3400 🚇 Brown, Red lines: Belmont 🚌 77

COURTYARD BY MARRIOTT
Large, comfortable, well-priced rooms, designed to meet the needs of business travellers. The Loop is within easy reach.
🏠 G5 ✉ 30 E Hubbard Street ☎ 800/321 2211 or 312/329 2500 🍽 Reasonable café (££) 🚇 Red line: Grand 🚌 36

THE KNICKERBOCKER
Built in 1927, and now renovated, this hotel stands close to the southern end of the Magnificent Mile. A secret stairwell on the 14th floor is a legacy of the Prohibition era.
🏠 H4 ✉ 163 E Walton Street ☎ 800/621 8140 or 312/751 8100 🍽 Good restaurant and café (££) 🚇 Red line: Chicago 🚌 36

LENOX SUITES
Well-appointed, all-suites hotel, with excellent rates in the pricey Rush Street area.
🏠 H5 ✉ 616 N Rush Street ☎ 800/44 LENOX or 312/337 1000 🍽 Good restaurant (££) 🚇 Red line: Grand 🚌 3, 11, 125, 145, 146, 147, 151

THE RAPHAEL
Tremendous value in an otherwise costly district, just off the Magnificent Mile. Most of the rooms are suites equipped with refrigerators.
🏠 H4 ✉ 201 E Delaware Place ☎ 800/821 5343 or 312/943 5000 🚇 Red line: Chicago 🚌 145, 146, 147, 151

TALBOTT HOTEL
The Talbott was built in 1927 as an apartment block, and most of the rooms still have a kitchen. There is no restaurant, but the room-service menu is long.
🏠 H4 ✉ 20 E Delaware Place ☎ 800/621 8506 or 312/944 4970 🚇 Red line: Grand 🚌 36

Toll-free phone numbers

Many hotels can be contacted with a toll-free number. These are prefixed '800' and accessed by first dialling '1'. They can usually be dialled from anywhere in the US or Canada, although there is sometimes a different toll-free number for calls made within Illinois. Toll-free numbers can be dialled from the UK at the standard international rate.

BUDGET ACCOMMODATION

Bed and breakfast

Bed-and-breakfast inns offer an interesting alternative to hotels. They are typically Victorian homes fitted out in sumptuous style and filled with antiques. B&Bs span all price categories and are found in many areas of Chicago, with a particularly strong concentration in Oak Park. The Bed & Breakfast Chicago agency (✉ PO Box 14088, Chicago, Illinois 60614 ☎ 800/375 7084 or 312/951 0085) operates a reservation system; it handles properties that are usually centrally located.

THE AVENUE

Well-priced motel with no frills but clean, serviceable rooms, near Grant Park.
✚ H8 ✉ 1154 S Michigan Avenue ☎ 800/621 4196 or 312/427 8200 🚇 Orange line: Roosevelt 🚌 1, 3, 4, 38

BEST WESTERN RIVER NORTH

Good-value if unexciting rooms, and a rooftop pool. Close to the nightspots of River North.
✚ G5 ✉ 125 W Ohio Street ☎ 800/727 0800 or 312/467 0800 🍴 Reasonable restaurant (££) 🚇 Red line: Grand 🚌 22

THE CLARIDGE

Dating from the 1930s, this is a small hotel in the prosperous Gold Coast neighbourhood. Attractive weekend rates.
✚ G4 ✉ 1244 N Dearborn Street ☎ 800/245 1258 or 312/787 4980 🍴 Good restaurant (££) 🚇 Red line: Clark/Division 🚌 36

COMFORT INN

Unelaborate but perfectly adequate rooms at bargain prices; well north of the Loop but handy for Lincoln Park.
✚ F1 ✉ 601 W Diversey Parkway ☎ 800/221 2222 or 773/348 2810 🚇 Brown line: Diversey 🚌 76

DAYS INN LAKE SHORE DRIVE

Lake views are the big plus of this large, plain motel. Half the rooms have them; the other half have views of skyscrapers. Good value, and close to Navy Pier.
✚ J5 ✉ 644 N Lake Shore Drive ☎ 800/541 3223 or 312/943 9200 🍴 Ordinary restaurant (£–££) 🚇 Red line: Grand 🚌 3, 66, 157

HOSTEL CHICAGO INTERNATIONAL

A mixture of dormitory beds and double rooms, several miles north of the centre but with good public transport links. No age restrictions, but from Sunday to Thursday, for much of the year, you have to be back in the building by midnight. Curfew time is 2AM on weekends all year, and every night during the summer.
✚ Off map ✉ 6318 N Winthrop Avenue ☎ 773/262 1011 🚇 Red line: Loyola 🚌 155

OHIO HOUSE

Dependable, simple motel offering exceptional rates close to River North.
✚ G5 ✉ 600 N La Salle Street ☎ 312/943 6000 🍴 Adjoining coffee shop (£) 🚇 Red line: Grand 🚌 37, 41

THE SURF HOTEL

Great-value rooms on a residential street in the bohemian, increasingly fashionable Lake View neighbourhood. The building dates from the 1920s, and is full of character – the lobby is especially charming, with a fireplace and high windows. Not at the hub of the city, but fine for the lake, Lincoln Park, and numerous bars and restaurants.
✚ Off map ✉ 555 W Surf Street ☎ 773/528 8400 🚇 Brown line: Diversey 🚌 36

CHICAGO
travel facts

ARRIVING & DEPARTING

Before you go

- British citizens require a valid 10-year passport to visit the United States.
- A visa is required if:
  (1) you are staying more than 90 days;
  (2) your visit is not a holiday or business trip;
  (3) you have ever been refused a visa or refused admission to the United States, or have been required to leave the United States by the US Immigration and Naturalisation Service.
  (4) you do not have a return or onward ticket.
  A Visa Waiver form is supplied by the airline.
- To apply for a visa, or for more information, call the United States Embassy Visa Information Line ☎ 0891 200 2900
- No vaccinations are required to enter the United States unless you have come from, or stopped over in, countries where there are epidemics.

When to go

- June, July and August are the busiest months, but weather can be tryingly hot.
- May, September and October are better months to visit, with fewer crowds and warm but less extreme weather.
- Events and festivals take place year round (► 22). Most open-air events happen between spring and autumn.
- Major conventions cause hotel space to be scarce; August, September and October are peak convention months. Check ahead.

Climate

- Summers are hot and humid; winters are cold with snow; spring is mild but short; autumn is mild and pleasant – September, October and early November have the best weather.
- Be prepared for warm days and chilly evenings between April and October.
- Weather is changeable at any time; bring an umbrella and raincoat. Most rainfall is from April to September.
- The wind is always there. It comes off the lake, and is particularly brutal in winter.

Arriving by air

- Chicago's O'Hare International Airport is 17 miles north-west of the Loop. It handles all international flights and most domestic flights. Midway Airport is 8 miles south-west of the Loop: a quieter alternative for domestic flights.
- Continental Air Transport ☎ 312/454 7799 runs minibuses between O'Hare and the Loop every five minutes 6AM–11:30PM; fare $14.75. From Midway, minibuses to the Loop leave every 15–20 minutes; fare $10.50.
- Chicago Transit Authority ☎ 312/836 7000 runs Blue Line trains between O'Hare and the Loop around the clock. The trip takes around 35 minutes; fare $1.50. From Midway, Orange Line trains make the 30-minute journey to the Loop; fare $1.50. Late at night, take a cab.
- Taxis wait at the arrivals terminal at each airport. The fare to the Loop or nearby hotels is $25–$30 from O'Hare,

$20–$23 from Midway. A Shared-Ride option (from both airports) costs $15 each.

- Airport Information: O'Hare ☎ 312/686 2200 Midway ☎ 312/665 2385

Arriving by bus

- Greyhound buses into Chicago arrive at 630 W Harrison Street, six blocks southwest of the Loop. ☎ 800/231 2222 or 312/718 2900

Arriving by train

- Amtrak trains use Chicago's Union Station, junction of W Adams and S Canal streets, two blocks west of the Loop.
- Information ☎ 800/872 7245 or 312/558 1075

Arriving by car

- Chicago has good Interstate access: I-80 and I-90 are the major east–west routes; I-55 and I-57 arrive from the south. I-94 runs through the city linking the north and south suburbs.
- To reach the Loop from O'Hare airport use I-90/94. From Midway airport take I-55, linking with the northbound I-90/94 for the Loop. These journeys will take 45–90 minutes and 30–60 minutes respectively, according to traffic conditions.
- Avoid arriving during the rush hours, 7–9AM and 4–7PM.
- Many hotels have guest car parks, otherwise overnight parking is difficult and very costly. During the day, street parking is often limited to two hours; spaces in the Loop are near impossible to find.
- Driving in the city is stressful: use public transport.

Customs regulations

- Duty-free allowances include 32fl oz alcoholic spirits or wine (no one under 21 may bring alcohol into the US), 200 cigarettes or 50 cigars, and up to $100-worth of gifts.
- Some medication bought over the counter abroad may be prescription-only in the US and may be confiscated. Bring a doctor's certificate for essential medication.

Departure and airport tax

- These are included in the cost of your plane ticket.

ESSENTIAL FACTS

Travel insurance

- Travel insurance is strongly recommended. Comprehensive insurance, which should include medical cover of at least £1,000,000, costs £30–£45 per person for a seven-day stay.

Usual opening hours

- Shops: Mon–Sat from 9 or 10 until 5 or 6. Most shops are also open Sun noon–5. Department stores and malls keep longer hours; many bookshops open in the evenings.
- Banks: Mon–Fri from 8 or 9 to 3, 4 or 5, with some branches open later once a week.

National holidays

- New Year's Day (1 Jan)
- Martin Luther King Day (third Mon in Jan)
- President's Day (third Mon in Feb)
- Memorial Day (last Mon in May)
- Independence Day (4 July)

- Labor Day (first Mon in Sep)
- Columbus Day (second Mon in Oct)
- Veteran's Day (11 Nov)
- Thanksgiving Day (fourth Thu in Nov)
- Christmas Day (25 Dec)

Money matters
- The unit of currency is the dollar (= 100 cents). Notes (bills) come in $1, $5, $10, $20, $50 and $100 denominations; coins are 25¢ (a quarter), 10¢ (a dime), 5¢ (a nickel) and 1¢ (a penny). Less common are $1 coins.
- Most banks have Automatic Teller Machines (ATMs), which accept credit cards registered in other countries that are linked to the Cirrus or Plus networks. Ensure your personal identification number is valid in the US: four- and six-figure numbers are usual.
- Credit cards are widely accepted.
- US dollar traveller's cheques function like cash in most shops; $20 and $50 denominations are most useful. Seeking to exchange these (or foreign currency) at a bank can be difficult and commissions can be high.
- An 8.75 per cent sales tax is added to marked retail prices, except on groceries and prescription drugs.

Etiquette
- Smoking is banned in all public buildings and transportation, and in cinemas. It is also banned or restricted in many hotels and restaurants.
- Tipping is voluntary, but the following are usually expected:

15 per cent-plus in restaurants; 15–20 per cent for taxis; $1 per bag for a hotel porter.

Solo travellers
- Solo travellers, including women, are not unusual.
- Women may encounter unwanted attention and, after dark, should avoid being alone on the street when not in established nightlife areas. If waiting for a cab, do so inside the club or restaurant, or where staff can see you.

Tourist offices
- Visitor Centers are: inside the Historic Water Tower ✉ 806 N Michigan Avenue ☎ 312/744 2400, at the Chicago Cultural Center, ✉ 77 E Randolph Street ☎ 312/744 2400, and at Illinois Market Place ✉ Navy Pier, 700 E Grand Avenue. All are open daily but may close on holidays.

Student travellers
- An International Student Identity Card (ISIC) reduces admission to many museums and other attractions.
- Anyone aged under 21 is forbidden to buy or drink alcohol and may be denied admission to some nightclubs.

Time differences
- Chicago is one hour behind the US's East Coast, two hours ahead of the US's West Coast, six hours behind the UK, seven hours behind Western Europe, and 14–16 hours behind Australia.

Public toilets
- Most department stores, malls and hotel lobbies have adequate toilets.

Electricity

- The supply is 110 volts; 60 cycles AC current.
- US appliances use two-prong plugs. European appliances require an adaptor.

PUBLIC TRANSPORT

- Much of Chicago can be explored on foot. To travel between neighbourhoods use the network of buses and El (elevated railway) trains, which travel above and below ground, and buses.
- El trains operate 24 hours a day but using trains or buses at night can be dangerous.
- Metra commuter trains are best for visiting some areas.
- For information on the El and buses:
  Chicago Transit Authority
  ☎ 312/836 7000
  Metra ☎ 312/322 6777 (🕐 Mon–Fri 8–5), otherwise 312/836 7000

The El

- Fare: $1.50. Transfer to a different line (or to a bus) within two hours: 30¢ (free within Loop). A second transfer within the same two hours is free.
- Plastic transit cards are the simplest way to pay fares. Tokens ($13.50 for ten) and cash are the alternatives.
- Transit cards – available in any value from $3–$100 – can also be used on buses and can be recharged later.
- Stations have fare booths or automatic ticket machines.
- Six colour-coded lines (➤ 6) run through the city and converge on the Loop.
- On weekdays 6AM–7PM, trains on most lines stop only at alternate stations, plus all major stations. Check in advance whether you need to take the A service or the B service.
- Most trains run 24 hours; frequency is reduced during weekends and late evenings.
- Some stations close at weekends.

Buses

- Fare: $1.50. Transfer to a different route (or to the El) within two hours: 30¢. Second transfer as for the El.
- As for the El, plastic transit cards are the simplest way to pay fares. Tokens (as for the El) and cash (exact change only) are the alternatives.

Schedule and map information

- CTA maps showing El and bus routes are available from El station fare booths.
- Bus routes are shown at stops.

Taxis

- Can be hailed, and wait outside hotels, conference centres and major El stations.
- Fares are $1.20 plus $1.20 per mile and 50¢ each for more than one passenger.
- Hotel, restaurant and nightclub staff will order a taxi on request; or you can phone the following firms:
  American United ☎ 312/248 7600
  Checker ☎ 312/243 2537
  Yellow ☎ 312/829 4222

MEDIA & COMMUNICATIONS

Telephones

- Public telephones are found in the street, and in hotel lobbies, restaurants and public buildings. Local calls cost 35¢.

- Calls from hotel rooms are usually more expensive than those from public phones.
- Many businesses have toll-free numbers, prefixed 800, allowing the public to phone them for free. First dial '1'.
- Most US phones use touch-tone dialling, enabling callers to access extensions directly.

Post offices
- Minimum charges for sending a postcard or letter overseas are 50¢ and 60¢ respectively.
- Main post office ✉ 433 W Van Buren Street. To find the nearest post office, look in the phone book or ask at your hotel. Most open Mon–Fri 8:30–5, Sat 8:30–1. ☎ 312/765 4357

Newspapers
- Major daily newspapers are the *Chicago Tribune* (international, national and local issues) and the tabloid *Chicago Sun-Times* (local stories). Best of several free weeklies is the *Chicago Reader*, with local news, features and entertainment listings.

Magazines
- Glossy monthly magazines such as *Chicago* reflect the interests of the well-heeled Chicagoan. *Windy City Times* is pitched at gays and lesbians. Free magazines such as *Chicago Key*, found in hotel lobbies, are aimed at tourists.

International newsagents
- Overseas newspapers and magazines can be found at Barnes & Noble and Borders Books & Music stores (▶ 75).

Radio
- Alternative rock: Q101 101FM, WXRT 93FM
- Classical: WFMT 98.7FM
- Country: WUSN 99.5FM
- Jazz: WNUA 95.5FM
- National Public Radio: WBEZ 91.5FM
- News: WBBM 780AM, WMAQ 670AM
- Rock: WCKG 105.9FM
- R&B: WGCI 107.5FM
- Talk radio and local sports: WGN 720AM

Television
- The main Chicago TV channels are 2 WBBM (CBS), 5 WMAQ (NBC), 7 WLS (ABC), 9 WPW (local independent), 11 WTTW (PBS).
- Most hotels offer cable TV and pay-per-view movies.

EMERGENCIES

Sensible precautions
- By day, the Loop and major areas of interest to visitors are relatively safe. Some tourist sites involve journeys through unwelcoming areas; be especially wary if travelling through the South Side and Near West Side. Discuss your itinerary with hotel staff and heed their advice.
- After dark, stick to established nightlife areas. River North and River West, Rush and Division streets, and Wrigleyville/Lake View are relatively safe if you take commonsense precautions. Public transport is generally safe between these areas, but be cautious.
- Neighbourhoods can change character within a few blocks. Stick to safe, busy streets.

- Carry shoulder bags strapped across your chest, and keep your wallet in your front trouser pocket or chest pocket. In a bar or restaurant, keep your belongings within sight and within reach.
- Store valuables in your hotel's safe and never carry more money than you need. Most major purchases can be made with travellers' cheques or credit cards.
- Lost travellers' cheques are relatively easy to replace. Read the instructions when you buy the cheques and carry the instructions with you – but keep them separate from the cheques.
- Replacing a stolen passport is tricky and begins with a visit or phone call to your country's nearest consular office.
- Report any item stolen to the nearest police precinct (address in the phone book). It is unlikely that any stolen goods will be recovered but the police will be able to fill in the forms which your insurance company needs.

Lost property

- O'Hare International Airport ☎ 312/686 2200
- Lost in a cab ☎ 312/744 2900 or 312/744 6227
- The El and buses: Chicago Transit Authority ☎ 312/836 7000; Metra ☎ 312/322 6777 (🕐 Mon–Fri 8–5), or 312/836 7000

Medical treatment

- For doctors, ask hotel staff or the non-emergency Medical Referral Service ☎ 312/670 2550

- In an emergency go to a hospital with a 24-hour emergency room, such as Northwestern Memorial Hospital ✉ 233 E Superior Street ☎ 312/908 2000
- The Chicago Dental Association ☎ 312/836 7300 will refer you to a dentist in your area.

Medicines

- Pharmacies are listed in *Yellow Pages*. Visitors from Europe will find many familiar medicines under unfamiliar names. Some drugs, available over the counter at home, are issued only with a prescription.
- If you use medication regularly, bring a supply (but note the warning given in Customs Regulations, ► 89). If you intend to buy prescription drugs in the US, bring a note from your doctor.
- Late-night pharmacies in the city include Walgreen's ✉ 757 N Michigan Avenue ☎ 800/925 4733 🕐 24 hours. Osco's Drugs has a toll-free number ☎ 800/654 6726 giving the location of its nearest 24-hour branch.

Emergency telephone numbers

- Fire, police or ambulance ☎ 911 (no money required)
- Rape Crisis Hotline ☎ 312/744 8418

Consulates

- Germany ✉ 676 N Michigan Avenue, Suite 3200 ☎ 312 580 1199
- Ireland ✉ 400 N Michigan Avenue, Room 911 ☎ 312/337 1868
- UK ✉ 33 N Dearborn Street ☎ 312/346 1810

INDEX

CityPack
Chicago

Written by   Mick Sinclair
Edited, designed and produced by
    [AA] Publishing

Maps   © The Automobile Association 1997, 1999
Fold-out map © RV Reise- und Verkehrsverlag Munich · Stuttgart
      © Cartography: GeoData

Distributed in the United Kingdom by AA Publishing, Norfolk House, Priestley Road,
Basingstoke, Hampshire, RG24 9NY.

The contents of this publication are believed correct at the time of printing. Nevertheless, the
publishers cannot be held responsible for any errors or omissions or for changes in the details
given in this guide or for the consequences of any reliance on the information provided by the
same. Assessments of attractions, hotels, restaurants and so forth are based upon the author's
own personal experience and, therefore, descriptions given in this guide necessarily contain an
element of subjective opinion which may not reflect the publishers' opinion or dictate a
reader's own experiences on another occasion.
We have tried to ensure accuracy in this guide, but things do change and we would be grateful
if readers would advise us of any inaccuracies they may encounter.

Colour separation by Daylight Colour Art Pte Ltd, Singapore
Printed and bound by Dai Nippon Printing Co (Hong Kong) Ltd.

Acknowledgements
The Automobile Association wishes to thank the following libraries and institutes for their
assistance in the preparation of this book: Allsports (UK) Ltd (S Bruty) cover (main
picture); The Art Institute of Chicago 40b; The Bridgeman Art Library, London 36, scene
from 'The Last of the Mohicans' (New York Historical Society); Chicago Board of Trade
31a; Mary Evans Picture Library 12; The Glessner House Museum, courtesy of Prairie
Avenue House Museums, Chicago 43; Frank Lloyd Wright Home & Studio Foundation
24a, 24b; The Photographers Library cover (inset); The University of Chicago 47a, 47b
The remaining photographs are held in the Association's own library (AA Photo Library)
and were taken by Phil Wood with the exception of page 56 taken by Sean M. Taylor.

ORIGINAL COPY-EDITOR *Antonia Hebbert*   INDEXER: *Marie Lorimer*
REVISION VERIFIER: *Mick Sinclair*
SECOND EDITION UPDATED BY *OutHouse Publishing Services*

Titles in the Citypack series
● Amsterdam ● Atlanta ● Bangkok ● Barcelona ● Beijing ● Berlin ● Boston ●
● Brussels & Bruges ● Chicago ● Dublin ● Florence ● Hong Kong ● Istanbul ●
● Lisbon ● London ● Los Angeles ● Madrid ● Miami ● Montréal ● Moscow ●
● Munich ● New York ● Paris ● Prague ● Rome ● San Francisco ● Seattle ●
● Singapore ● Shanghai ● Sydney ● Tokyo ● Toronto ● Venice ● Vienna ●
● Washington D.C. ●